THE STORY OF A
GREAT SCHOOLMASTER

¶ Mr. Wells has also written the following novels:

THE WHEELS OF CHANCE
LOVE AND MR. LEWISHAM
KIPPS
TONO BUNGAY
ANN VERONICA
MR. POLLY
THE NEW MACHIAVELLI
MARRIAGE
THE PASSIONATE FRIENDS
THE WIFE OF SIR ISAAC HARMAN
BEALBY
THE RESEARCH MAGNIFICENT
MR. BRITLING SEES IT THROUGH
THE SOUL OF A BISHOP
JOAN AND PETER
THE UNDYING FIRE
THE SECRET PLACES OF THE HEART

¶ The following fantastic and imaginative romances:

THE TIME MACHINE
THE WONDERFUL VISIT
THE ISLAND OF DR. MOREAU
THE INVISIBLE MAN
THE WAR OF THE WORLDS
THE SLEEPER AWAKES
THE FIRST MEN IN THE MOON
THE SEA LADY
THE FOOD OF THE GODS
IN THE DAYS OF THE COMET
THE WAR IN THE AIR
THE WORLD SET FREE
MEN LIKE GODS
And numerous Short Stories published in several different collections

¶ A Series of books upon Social, Religious and Political questions:

ANTICIPATIONS (1900)
MANKIND IN THE MAKING
FIRST AND LAST THINGS
NEW WORLDS FOR OLD
A MODERN UTOPIA
THE FUTURE IN AMERICA
AN ENGLISHMAN LOOKS AT THE WORLD
WHAT IS COMING?
WAR AND THE FUTURE
IN THE FOURTH YEAR
GOD THE INVISIBLE KING
RUSSIA IN THE SHADOWS
THE SALVAGING OF CIVILIZATION
WASHINGTON AND THE RIDDLE OF PEACE
THE OUTLINE OF HISTORY
A SHORT HISTORY OF THE WORLD

¶ And two little books about children's play, called:

FLOOR GAMES and LITTLE WARS

F. W. Sanderson

THE
STORY OF A GREAT
SCHOOLMASTER

BY

H. G. WELLS

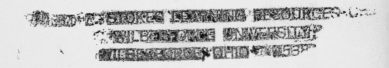

𝔑𝔢𝔴 𝔜𝔬𝔯𝔨

THE MACMILLAN COMPANY
1924

Printed in the United States of America by
THE FERRIS PRINTING COMPANY, NEW YORK

CONTENTS

CHAPTER I

v

LIST OF ILLUSTRATIONS

THE STORY OF A
GREAT SCHOOLMASTER

THE STORY OF A GREAT SCHOOLMASTER

CHAPTER I

SANDERSON THE MAN

§ 1

OF all the men I have met—and I have now had a fairly long and active life and have met a very great variety of interesting people—one only has stirred me to a biographical effort. This one exception is F. W. Sanderson, for many years the headmaster of Oundle School. I think him beyond question the greatest man I have ever known with any degree of intimacy, and it is in the hope of conveying to others something of my sense not merely of his importance, but of his peculiar genius and the rich humanity of his character, that I am setting out to write this book. He was in himself a very delightful mixture of subtlety and simplicity, generosity, adventurousness, imagination and steadfast purpose, and he approached the general life of our time at such an angle as to reflect the most curious and profitable lights upon it.   To tell his story is to reflect upon all the main educational ideas of the last half-century, and to revise our conception of the process and purpose of the modern community in relation to education.   For Sanderson had a mind like an octopus, it seemed always to have a tentacle free to reach out beyond what was already held, and his tentacles grew and radiated farther and farther.   Before his end he had come to a vision of the school as a centre for the complete reorganisation of civilised life.

I knew him personally only during the last eight years of his life; I met him for the first time in 1914, when I was proposing to send my sons to his school.   But our thoughts and interests drew us very close to one another, I never missed an opportunity of meeting and talking to him, and I was the last person he spoke to before his sudden death.   He was sixty-six years of age when he died.   Those last eight years were certainly the richest and most productive of his whole career;

he grew most in those years; he travelled farthest.
I think I saw all the best of him. It is, I think,
no disadvantage to have known him only in his
boldest and most characteristic phase. It saves
me from confusion between his maturer and his
earlier phases. He was a much stratified man.
He had grown steadfastly all his life, he had
shaken off many habitual inhibitions and freed
himself from once necessary restraints and limitations. He would go discreetly while his convic-
tions accumulated and then break forward very
rapidly. He had a way of leaving people behind,
and if I had fallen under his spell earlier, I, too,
might have been left far behind. He was, I
recall, a rock-climber; he was a mental rock-
climber also, and though he was very wary of
recalcitrance, there were times when his pace became so urgent that even his staff and his own
family were left tugging, breathless and per-
plexed, at the rope.

Out of a small country grammar-school he
created something more suggestive of those great
modern teaching centres of which our world
stands in need than anything else that has yet
been attempted. By all ordinary standards the

Oundle School of his later years was a brilliant success; it prospered amazingly, there was an almost hopeless waiting-list of applicants; boys had to be entered five years ahead; but successful as it was, it was no more than a sketch and demonstration of the great schools that are yet to be. I saw my own sons get an education there better than I had ever dared hope for them in England, but from the first my interest in the intention and promise of Oundle went far beyond its working actualities. And all the educational possibilities that I had hitherto felt to be unattainable dreams, matters of speculation, things a little too extravagant even to talk about in our dull age, I found being pushed far towards realisation by this bold, persistent, humorous and most capable man.

Let me first try to give you a picture of his personality as he lives in my memory. Then I will try to give an account of his beginnings, as far as I have been able to learn about them, and so we will come to our main theme, *Sanderson contra Mundum*, the schoolmaster who set out to conquer the world. For, as I shall show, that and no less was what he was trying to do in the last years of his life.

'Ruddy' and 'jolly' are the adjectives that come first to mind when I think of describing him. He had been a slender, energetic young man his early photographs witness; but long before I met him he had become plump and energetic, with a twinkling appreciation for most of the good things of life. His complexion had a reddish fairness; he had well-modelled features, thick eyebrows and thick moustache touched with grey, and he wore spectacles through and over and beside which his active eyes took stock of you. About his eyes were kindly wrinkles, and generally I remember him as smiling—often with a touch of roguery in the smile. Quick movements of his head caused animating flashes of his glasses. He was carrying a little too much body for his heart, and that made him short of breath. His voice was in his chest, there was a touch of his native Northumbria in his accent, and he had a habit of speaking in incomplete sentences with a frequent use of the interrogative form. His manner was confidential; he would bend towards his hearer and drop his voice a little. 'Now what do you think of ——?' he would say, or 'I've been thinking of ——' so and so. At times his confidential manner became endearingly suggestive of a friendly conspirator. This, as yet, he seemed to say, was not for too careless a publication. You and he understood, but those other fellows—they were difficult fellows. It might not be practicable to attempt everything at once.

That reservation, that humorous discretion, is very essential in my memory of him. It is essential to the whole educational situation of the world. He was an exceptionally bold and creative man, and he was a schoolmaster, and that is perhaps as near as one can come to a complete incompatibility of quality and conditions. In no part of our social life is dull traditionalism so powerfully entrenched as it is in our educational organisation. We have still to realise the evil of mental heaviness in scholastic concerns. We take, very properly, the utmost precautions to exclude men and women of immoral character not only from actual teaching but also from any exercise of educational authority. But no one ever makes the least objection to the far more deadly influences of stupidity and unteachable ignorance. Our conceptions of morality are still grossly physical. The heavier and slower a man's mind seems to be, the more addicted he is to intellectual narcotics, the more people trust him as a schoolmaster. He will 'stay put.'

A timid obstructiveness is the atmosphere in which almost all educational effort has to work, and schoolmasters are denied a liberty of thought and speech conceded to every other class of respectable men. They must still be mealy-mouthed about Darwin, fatuously conventional in politics, and emptily orthodox in religion. If they stimulate their boys they must stimulate as a brass trumpet does, without words or ideas. They may be great leaders of men—provided they lead backwards or nowhither. Sanderson in his latter days broke into unexampled freedom, but for the greater part of his life he was—like most of his profession—'wading hips-deep in fools,' and equally resolved to work out his personal impulse and retain the great opportunities that the governing body of Oundle School had, almost unwittingly, put into his hands. He was therefore not only a great revolutionary but something of a Vicar of Bray. A large part of the amusing subtlety of his personality was the result of the balanced course he had to pursue. In all

he did, in all he said, he was feeling his way.
No other schoolmaster——and there must be many
a rebellious heart lying still in the graves of dead
schoolmasters and many a stifled rebel in the
schoolrooms of to-day—no other schoolmaster has
ever felt his way so discreetly, so far and, at last,
so triumphantly.

I remember as a very characteristic thing that
he said one day when I asked for his opinion of a
particularly progressive and hopeful addition to
his board of governors: 'He does not know much
about schools yet, but he will learn.   Oundle will
teach him.'   And in his last great lecture, he flung
out a general 'aside'——that lecture was full of
astonishing 'asides'——'I turned round on the boys
and the parents,' he said, *both are my business.*'

Never was schoolmaster so emancipated as he
in his latter years from the ancient servility of the
pedagogue.   Not for him the handing on of mel-
low traditions and genteel gestures of the mind,
not for him the obedient administration of useful
information to employers' sons by the docile em-
ployee.   He saw the modern teacher in university and school plainly for what he has to be, the
anticipator, the planner, and the foundation-

maker of the new and greater order of human life that arises now visibly amidst the decaying structures of the old.

§ 2

Sanderson was born and brought up outside the British public-school system that he was to affect so profoundly. His early education was obtained in a parish school. His father was employed in the estate office of Lord Boyne at Brancepeth in Durham. There were several brothers but they all died before manhood, and the scanty indications one can glean of those early years suggest a slender, studious, and probably rather delicate youngster. He was never very proficient in any out-of-door games. In the early days at Oundle he careered about on a bicycle; in later years he played tennis; his vacation exercise was rock-scrambling. He became a 'student-teacher,' so the official Life phrases it, at a school at Tudhoe, but whether there was any difference between being a student-teacher at a school at Tudhoe and being an ordinary pupil-teacher in an ordinary elementary school under the English Education

Department I have been unable to ascertain. He was already notable in his village world as exceptionally intelligent, industrious, and ambitious, and with a little encouragement from the local vicar and one or two friends he effected an escape from the strangling limitations of elementary teaching.

He may have aimed at the church at that time. At any rate he gained a scholarship and entered Durham University as a theological student. He did well in Durham University both in theology and mathematics; he was made a Fellow and he was able to go on as a scholar from Durham to the wider and more strenuous academic life of Cambridge. At Cambridge theology drops out of the foreground of the picture. He took a fairly good degree in mathematics, and he worked for the Natural Science Tripos. He did not fight his way up into that select class which secures Cambridge fellowships, but he had made a reputation as an able, hard, and honest worker; he was much sought after as a coach, and he was given a lectureship in the woman's college of Girton. From this he went as senior physics master to the big school for boys at Dulwich.

A photograph of him in the early Dulwich period shows him slender and keen-looking, already bespectacled and with a thick moustache; except for the glasses not unlike another ruddy north-countryman I once knew, the novelist George Gissing. Both were what one might call Scandinavian in type. But Gissing was as despondent as Sanderson was buoyant. In those days, an old Dulwich associate tells me, Sanderson was in a state of great mental fermentation. He loved long walks in his spare time, and along the pebbly paths and roads and up and down the little hills of that corner of Kent, the two of them talked out a hundred aspects and issues of the perplexing changing world in which they found themselves.

It was the world of the eighteen-eighties they were looking at, before the first Jubilee of Queen Victoria, and it may be worth while to devote a paragraph or so to a reconstruction of the moral and intellectual landscape this lean and eager young man was confronting.

Upon the surface and in its general structure that British world of the eighties had a delusive air of final establishment. Queen Victoria had been reigning for close upon half a century and seemed likely to reign for ever. The economic system of unrestricted private enterprise with privately owned capital had yielded a great harvest of material prosperity, and few people suspected how rapidly it was exhausting the soil of willing service in which it grew. Production increased every year; population increased every year; there was a steady progress of invention and discovery, comfort, and convenience. Wars went on, a marginal stimulation of the empire, but since the collapse of Napoleon I. no war had happened to frighten England for its existence as a country; no threat of warfare that could touch English life or English soil troubled men's imagination. Ruskin and Carlyle had criticised English ideals and the righteousness of English commerce and industrialism, but they were regarded generally as eccentric and unaccountable men; there was already a conflict of science and theology, but it affected the national life very little outside the world of the intellectuals; a certain amount of trade competition from the United States and from other European countries was developing, but at most it ruffled the surface of

the national self-confidence. There was a social-
ist movement, but it was still only a passionless
criticism of trade and manufacturers, a criticism
poised between aesthetic fastidiousness and be-
nevolence. People played with that Victorian
socialism as they would have played with a very
young tiger-cub. The labour movement was a
gentle insistence upon rather higher wages and
rather shorter hours; it had still to discover Socialism. In a world of certainties the rate of
interest fell by minute but perceptible degrees,
and as a consequence money for investment went
abroad until all the world was under tribute to
Britain. History seemed to be over, entirely
superseded by the daily paper; tragedy and catastrophe were largely eliminated from human life.
One read of famines in India and civil chaos in
China, but one felt that these were diminishing
distresses; the missionaries were at work there and
railways spreading.

It was indeed a mild and massive Sphynx of
British life that confronted our young man at
Dulwich and his friend, an amoeboid Sphynx
which enveloped and assimilated rather than tore
and devoured. It had not been stricken for a

generation, and so it felt assured of the ages.
But beneath its tranquil-looking surfaces many
ferments were actively at work, and its serene
and empty visage masked extensive processes of
decay. The fifty-year-old faith on which the
social and political fabric rested—for all social
and political fabrics must in the last resort rest
upon faith—was being corroded and dissolved
and removed. Britain in the mid-Victorian time
stood strong and sturdy in the world because a
great number of its people, its officials, employers,
professional men and workers honestly believed
in the rightness of its claims and professions, believed in its state theology, in the justice of its
economic relationships, in the romantic dignity
of its monarchy, and in the real beneficence and
righteousness of its relations to foreigners and the
subject-races of the Empire. They did what they
understood to be their duty in the light of that
belief, simply, directly, and with self-respect and
mutual confidence. If some of its institutions fell
short of perfection, few people doubted that they
led towards it. But from the middle of the
century onward this assurance of the prosperous
British in their world was being subjected to a

more and more destructive criticism, spreading
slowly from intellectual circles into the general
consciousness.

It is interesting to note one or two dates in relation to Sanderson's life.   He was born in the year
1857.   This was two years before the publication
of Darwin's *Origin of Species*.   He was growing
up through boyhood as the application of the
Darwinian criticism of life to current theology
was made, and as the great controversy between
Science and orthodox beliefs came to a head.
Huxley's ʲchallenging book, *Man's Place in
Nature*, was published in 1863; Darwin became
completely explicit about human origins only in
1871 with *The Descent of Man*.   Sanderson, then
a bright and forward boy of fourteen, was probably already beginning to take notice of these
disputes about the fundamentals, as they were
then considered, of sound Christianity.

He was already at college when Huxley was
pounding Gladstone and the Duke of Argyll upon
such issues as whether the first chapter of Genesis
was strictly parallel with the known course of
evolution, and whether the miracle of the Gadarene swine was a just treatment of the Gadarene

swineherds. Sanderson's Durham and Cambridge studies and talks went on amidst the thunder of these debates, and there can be little doubt that his early theology underwent much bending and adaptation to the new realisations of the past of man, and of human destiny that these discussions opened out. He did not take holy orders but he remained in the Anglican Church; manifestly he could still find a meaning in the Fall and in the scheme of Salvation. Many other promising teachers of his generation found this impossible; such men as Graham Wallas, for example, felt compelled for conscience'-sake to abandon the public-school teaching to which they had hoped to give their lives. Wallas found scope for his very great gifts of suggestion and inspiration in the London School of Economics, but many others of these Victorian non-jurors were lost to education altogether.

The criticism of the economic life and social organisation of that age was going on almost parallel with the destruction of its cosmogony. Ruskin's *Unto this Last* was issued when Sanderson was four years old; *Fors Clavigera* was appearing in the seventies and the early eighties.

William Morris was a little later with *News from Nowhere* and *The Dream of John Ball;* they must have still been vividly new books in Sanderson's Cambridge days. Marx was little heard of then in England. He was already a power in German socialism in the seventies, but he did not reach the reader of English until the eighties were nearly at an end. When Sanderson discussed socialism during those Dulwich walks, it must have been Ruskin and Morris rather than Marx who figured in his talk. Although there remains no account of those early conversations, it is easy to guess that this stir of social reconstruction and religious readjustment must have played a large part in them. Sanderson meant to teach and wanted to teach; he was quite unlike that too common sort of schoolmaster who has fallen back into teaching after the collapse of other ambitions; like all really sincere teachers he was eager to learn, open to every new and stimulating idea, and free altogether from the malignant conservatism of the disappointed type.

He kept that adolescent power of mental growth throughout life. I remember my pleased astonishment on my first visit to Oundle to find in his library—I had drifted to his bookshelves while I awaited him—a row of the works of Nietzsche (who came into the English-speaking world in the late nineties) and recent books by Bertrand Russell and Shaw. Here was a schoolmaster, a British public schoolmaster, aware that the world was still going on! It seemed too good to be true. But it was true, and in the end Sanderson was to die, ten years, shall we say?— or twenty, ahead of his time.

And while we are placing Sanderson in relation to the intellectual stir of the age let us note, too, the general shape of human affairs as it was presented to his mind. It was an age of steadily accelerated political change, and of a vast increase in the population of the world. The fifties and sixties of the nineteenth century had seen the world-wide spread of the railway and telegraph network, and a consequent opening up of vast regions of production that had hitherto lain fallow. The screw was replacing the ineffective paddle-wheel of the earlier steamships and revolutionising ocean transport. There was a great increase in mechanical and agricultural efficiency. We still call that time the mid-Victorian period, but the history teacher of the future, more sensible than we are of the innocence of good Queen Victoria in any concern of importance to mankind, is more likely to distinguish it as the Advent of the New Communications. These new inventions were 'abolishing distance.' They were demanding a political synthesis of mankind. But there was little understanding as yet of this now manifest truth. One hardly notes a sign of any such awareness in literature and public discussions until the end of the century; and failing a clear understanding of their nature the new expansive forces operated through the cheap and unsound interpretations first of sentimental nationalism and then of romantic imperialism.

Sanderson's boyhood saw the differences of the cultures of north and south in the United States of America at first exacerbated by the new means of communication and then, after four years of civil war, resolved into a stabler unity. The straggling peninsula of Italy under the sway of the new synthetic forces recovered a unity it had lost with the decay of the Roman roads; the internal tension of the continental powers culminated in the Franco-German war. But these were insufficient adjustments, and a renewed growth of armaments upon land and sea alike, betrayed the growing mutual pressure of the great powers. All dreamt of expansion and none of coalescence. The dominant political fact in Europe while Sanderson was a young man, was the rise of Germany to political and economic predominance. German energy, restrained from geographical release, drove upward along the lines of scientific and technical progress, and the outward thrust of its pent-up imperialism took the form of a gathering military threat. Germany first and then the United States, released and renewed after their escape from the fragmentation that had threatened them, made the economic pace for the rest of the world throughout the eighties and the nineties. They stirred the British manufacturer and parent to indignant inquiries; they forced the drowsy schools of Great Britain into a reluctant admission of scientific and technical teaching. But they awakened as yet no profounder heart-searchings.

The young science-master at Dulwich talked, no doubt, as we all did in those days, of Evolution and Socialism, of the rights of labour and the Christianisation of industry, of the progress of science and the scandal of the increasing expenditure upon armaments, with the illusion of an immense general stability in the background of his mind. It was an illusion that needed not only the Great War of 1914-18 but its illuminating sequelae to shatter and destroy.

§ 3

Accounts of Sanderson's work in Dulwich school differ very widely. At one time it would seem that he had troubles about discipline, and it is quite conceivable that his methods there were experimental and fluctuating. No doubt he was trying over at Dulwich many of the things that were to establish his success at Oundle. On the whole the Dulwich work was good work, and it gave him sufficient reputation to secure the headmastership of Oundle School when presently the governing body of that school sought a man of energy and character to modernise it.

The most valuable result of his Dulwich period was the demonstration of the interestingness of practical work in physical science for boys who remained apathetic under the infliction of the stereotyped classical curriculum. He was not getting the pick of the boys there but the residue, but he was getting an alertness and interest out of this second-grade material that surprised even himself. The interest of the classical teaching was largely the interest of a spirited competition which demanded not only a special sort of literary ability but a special sort of competitive disposition. But there are quite clever boys of an amiable type to whom competition does not appeal, and some of these were among the most interesting of the youngsters who were awakened to industrious work by his laboratory instruction.

It is clear that before Sanderson went to Oundle he had already developed a firm faith in the possibility of a school with a new and more varied curriculum, in which a far greater proportion of the boys could be interested in their work than was the case in the contemporary classical and (formal) mathematical school, and also that he had conceived the idea of replacing the competitive motive, which had ruled the schools of Europe since the establishment of the great Jesuit schools three hundred years before, by the more vital stimulus of interest in the work itself. He also took to Oundle a proved and tested conception of the need for the utmost possible personal participation by every boy in every collective function of the school. Quite early in his Oundle career he came into conflict with his boys and carried his point upon the issue whether every boy was to sing in the school singing or whether that was to be left to the specialised choir of boys who had voices and a taste for that sort of thing. That was an essential issue for him. From the very first he was working for the rank and file and against the star system of school work by which a few boys sing or work or play with distinction and encouragement, against a background of neglected shirkers and defeated and discouraged competitors.

Sanderson married soon after he went to Dulwich. His wife came from Cumberland and she excelled in all those domestic matters that make a successful headmaster's wife. Throughout all the rest of his life she was his loyal and passionate partisan. His friends were her friends, and his critics and opponents were her enemies, and if she had a fault it was that she found it difficult to forgive any one who had seemed ever to differ from him.   Two sons were born during the seven years that passed in the little home in Dulwich. It must have been a very brisk and happy little home.   One can imagine the tall young man with his gown a little powdered with blackboard chalk, flying out behind him, striding along the school corridors to some fresh and successful experiment in laboratory work, or in homely tweeds walking along the Kentish lanes with his friend, or snatching a delightful half-hour in the nursery to see Master Roy's first attempts to walk, or reading some new and stirring book with the lamp of those days before electric lighting at his elbow. He was thirty-five when he achieved his last step in the upward career of a secondary schoolmaster and was appointed headmaster of Oundle.   That success probably came as a surprise, for Sanderson's modest origins and the fact that he was not in holy orders must have been a serious handicap upon his application.   It must have been a very elated young couple who packed their household belongings for the unknown town of Oundle.

CHAPTER II

THE MODERNISATION OF OUNDLE SCHOOL

§ 1

OUNDLE SCHOOL, which was to be the material of Sanderson's life work, which was to teach him so much and profit so richly by the reaction, was one of comparatively old standing. It was a pre-reformation foundation; a certain Joan Wyatt having endowed a schoolmaster in the place in 1485. Its main revenues, however, derived from Sir William Laxton, Lord Mayor of London and Master of the Grocers' Company, who in 1556 left considerable property to that body on condition that it supported a school in his native town of Oundle. The Grocers' Company took over the Joan Wyatt school and schoolmaster, and has discharged its obligations to Oundle with intermittent energy and honesty to this day.

Oundle has always been a school of fluctuating

fortunes.   The district round and about does not sustain a sufficient population to maintain full classes and an efficient staff, and only when the prestige of the school was great enough to attract boys from a distance had it any chance of flourishing.   Time after time an energetic head with more or less support from the distant governing body would push it into prominence and prosperity only to pass away and leave it to an equally rapid decline.   The London Grocers' Company is a very unsuitable body for educational work.   It is not organised for any such work.   It was originally a chartered association of city wholesalers, spice-dealers, and so forth, who maintained a certain standard of honest trading and protected their common interests in the middle ages; it commended itself to the spiritual care of St. Anthony, and built a great hall and acted as almoner for its impoverished members and their widows and orphans; its normal function to-day is the entertainment of princes and politicians.   It is now a fortuitous collection of merchants, business-men, and prosperous persons, and it is only by chance that now and then a group of its members have had the conscience and intelligence to rise above the normal indifference of such people to the full possibilities of the Laxton bequest.   Generally the Company's conduct of the school has varied between half-hearted help and negligence and the diversion of the funds to other ends; it has no tradition of competent governorship, and the ups and downs of Oundle have been dependent mainly upon the personal qualities of the masters who have chanced to be appointed.

There was a period of prosperity during the second quarter of the seventeenth century which was brought to an end by the plague, and by the impoverishment of the school through the fire of London in which various Laxton properties were destroyed.   Throughout a large part of the eighteenth century the school was completely effaced, and the entire revenues of the Laxton bequest were no doubt expended in hospitality. There was a revival in 1796.   In the seventies of the nineteenth century the school was doing well in mathematics under a certain Dr. Stansbury, and in the eighties it had as many as two hundred boys under the Rev. H. St. J. Reade. Then it declined again until the numbers sank below a hundred.   It was a time of quickened

consciences in educational matters, and some of
the more energetic and able members of the
Grocers' Company determined to make a drastic
change of conditions at Oundle.   They found
Sanderson ready to their hands.

§ 2

The world is changing so rapidly that it may be
well to say a few words about the type of school
Sanderson was destined to renovate.   Even in
the seventies and eighties these smaller 'classical'
schools had a quaint old-fashioned air amidst the
surrounding landscape.   They were staffed by the
less vigorous men of the university-scholar type;
men of the poorer educated classes in origin, not
able enough to secure any of the prizes reserved
for university successes, and not courageous
enough to strike out into the great world on their
own account.   They protected themselves from
the sense of inferiority by an exaggeration of the
value of the schooling and disciplines through
which they had gone, and they ignored their lack
of grasp in a worship of the petty accuracies
within their capacity.   Their ambition soared at

its highest to holy orders and a headmastership, a comfortable house, a competent wife, dignity, security, ease, and a certain celebrity in equation-dodging or the imitation of Latin and Greek compositions. Contemporary life and thought these worthy dominies regarded with a lofty scorn. The formal mathematical work, it is true, was not older than a century or a century and a half, but the classical training had come down in an unbroken tradition from the seventeenth century. One of the staff of Oundle when Sanderson took it over is described as a 'wonderful' classical master. 'His master passion,' we are told, 'for Latin elegiacs and Greek iambics fired many of his pupils, whose best efforts were copied into a book that bore the title *Inscribatur*.' These exercises in stereotyped expression were going on at Oundle right into the eighteen-nineties. They had their justification. From the school the boys passed on to the Universities of Oxford and Cambridge, where sympathetic examining authorities awarded the greater prizes at their disposal to the more proficient of these victims. The Civil Service Commissioners by a mark-rigging system that would have won the respect of an American election boss, kept the Higher Division of the Civil Service as a preserve for ignorance 'classically' adorned. So that the school could boast of 'an almost uninterrupted stream of scholarship successes at Cambridge' even in its decline in the late eighties, when its real educational value to the country it served was a negative quantity.

This seventeenth century 'classical' grind constituted the main work of the school, and no other subject seems to have been pursued with any industry. Most of the staff could not draw or use their hands properly; like most secondary teachers of that time they were innocent of educational science, and no attempt was made to teach every boy to draw. Drawing was still regarded as a 'gift' in those days. The normally intelligent boy without the peculiar aptitudes and plasticity needed to take Latin elegiacs seriously, had no educational alternative whatever. There was no mathematical teaching beyond low-grade formal stuff of a very boring sort, and the only science available was a sort of science teaching put in to silence the complaints of progressive-minded parents rather than with any educational intention, science teaching that was very properly called 'stinks.' It was a stinking imposture. The boy of good ordinary quality was driven therefore to games or 'hobbies' or mischief as an outlet for his energies, as chance might determine. The school buildings before Sanderson was appointed were as cramped as the curriculum; old boys recall the 'redolent' afternoon class-rooms; the Grocers' Company in its wisdom had built a new School-House during the brief boom under St. John Reade, between a public house on either side and a slum at the back. It must have been pleasant for master and boys alike to escape from the stuffiness of general teaching upon these premises, and from the priggish exploits in versification of the 'inspired' minority, to the cricket field. There one had scope; there was life. The Rev. H. St. J. Reade, the headmaster in the eighties, had been Captain of the Oxford Eleven, and drove the ball hard and far, to the admiration of all beholders.

The Rev. Mungo J. Park, who immediately preceded Sanderson, is described as a man of considerable personal dignity, aloof and leisurely, and greatly respected by the boys. Under him the number of the boys in the school declined to fewer than a hundred. That dwindling band led the normal life of boys at any small public school in England. Most of them were frightfully bored by the teaching of the bored masters; the wonderful classical master lashed himself periodically up to the infectious level of enthusiasm for his amazing exercises; there was cribbing and ragging and loafing, festering curiosities and emotional experimenting, and, thank Heaven! games a fellow could understand. If these boys learnt anything of the marvellous new vision of the world that modern science was unfolding, they learnt it by their own private reading and against the wishes of their antiquated teachers. They learnt nothing in school of the outlook of contemporary affairs, nothing of contemporary human work, nothing of the social and economic system in which many of them were presently to play the part of captains. If they learnt anything about their bodies it was secretly, furtively, and dirtily. The gentlemen in holy orders upon the staff, and the sermons in the Oundle parish church, had made souls incredible. There has been much criticism of the devotion to games in these dens of mental dinginess, but games were the only honest and conclusive exercises to be found in them. From the sunshine and reality of the swimming-pool, the boats, the cricket or football field, the boys came back into the ill-ventilated class-rooms to pretend, or not even to pretend, an interest in languages not merely dead, but now, through a process of derivation and imitation from one generation to another, excessively decayed. The memory of school taken into after life from these establishments was a memory of going from games and sunshine and living interest into class-rooms of twilight, bad air, and sham enthusiasm for exhausted things.

§ 3

Sanderson made his application for the head-mastership of Oundle at an unusually favourable time. There were several men of exceptional enlightenment and intelligence upon the governing body of the school, and they were resolved to modernise Oundle thoroughly and well. To the innovators the very unorthodoxy of Sanderson's upbringing and qualifications was a recommendation, to their opponents they made him a shocking candidate, and the Grocers' Company was rent in twain over his application.   It requires a little effort nowadays for us to understand just how undesirable a candidate this spectacled young man from Dulwich must have appeared to many of the older and riper 'grocers.'

In the first place he was not in holy orders, and it was a fixed belief of many people—in spite of the fact that few of the clerically-ruled English public schools of that time could be described as hotbeds of chastity—that only clergymen in holy orders could maintain a satisfactory moral and religious tone.   On the other hand, he had been a distinguished theological student.   That, however, might involve heresy; English people have an instinctive perception of the corrosive effect of knowledge and intelligence upon sound dogma. Then he was not a public-school boy, and this might involve a loss of social atmosphere more important even than religion or morals.   The almost natural grace of deportment that has endeared the English traveller and the English official to the foreigner, and particularly to the subject-races throughout the world, might fail under his direction.   Moreover, he was no crick-

Interior in Science Block

eter. He had no athletic distinction; a terrible come-down after the Rev. H. St. J. Reade. These were all grave considerations in those days. Against them weighed the growing dread of German efficiency that was already spreading a wholesome modesty throughout the commercial world of Britain. This young man from Dulwich might bring to Oundle, it was thought, the base but valuable gifts of technical science. And there was apparent in him a liveliness and energy uncommon among scholastic applicants. His seemed to be a bracing personality, and Oundle was in serious need of a bracing régime. The members who liked him liked him warmly, and he roused prejudices as warm; feeling seems to have run high at the decision, and he was appointed by a majority of one.

The little world of Oundle heard of the new appointment with mixed and various feelings, in which there was no doubt a considerable amount of resentment. No man becomes headmaster of an established school without facing many difficulties. If he is promoted from among the staff of his predecessor old disputes and rivalries are apt to take on an exaggerated importance, and if he comes in from outside he finds a staff disposed to a meticulous defence of established usage. And the young couple from Dulwich came to the place in direct condemnation of its current condition and its best traditions. There can be no doubt that at the outset the school and town bristled defensively and unpleasantly to the newcomers.

In one respect the old educational order had a great advantage over the new that Sanderson was to inaugurate. It had a completed tradition, and it provided the standards by which the new was tried. Whatever it taught was held to be necessary to education, and all that it did not know was not knowledge. By such tests the equipment of Sanderson was exhibited as both defective and superfluous. Moreover, the new system was confessedly undeveloped and experimental. It could not be denied that Sanderson might be making blunders, and that he might have to retrace his steps. People had been teaching the classics for three centuries; the routine had become so mechanical that it was done best by men who were intellectually and morally half asleep. It led to nothing; except in very exceptional cases it did not even lead to a competent use of either the Latin or Greek languages; it involved no intelligent realisation of history, it detached the idea of philosophy from current life, and it produced the dreariest artistic Philistinism, but there was a universal persuasion that in some mystical way it *educated*. The methods of teaching science, on the other hand, were still in the experimental stage, and had still to convince the world that even at the lowest levels of failure they constituted a highly beneficent discipline.

I do not propose to disentangle here the story of Sanderson's first seven years of difficulty. He found the school and the town sullen and hostile, and he was young, eager, and irascible. The older boys had all been promoted upon classical qualifications, they were saturated with the old public-school tradition that Sanderson had come to destroy, and behind them were various members of a hostile and resentful staff inciting them to obstruction and mischief. Neither Mr. nor Mrs. Sanderson was old enough or wise enough to disregard slights or to ignore mere gestures of hostility.

Reminiscences of old boys in the official life

give us glimpses of the way in which the old order fought against the new. Everything was done to emphasise the fact that Sanderson was 'no gentleman,' 'no sportsman,' 'no cricketer,' 'no scholar.' It is the dearest delusion of snobs everywhere that able men who have made their way in the world are incapable of acquiring a valet's knowledge of what is correct in dress and deportment, and the dark legend was spread that he wore a flannel shirt with a sort of false front called a 'dicky' and detachable cuffs, in place of the evening shirt of the genteel. Moreover, his dress tie was reported to be a made-up tie. Unless he is to undress in public I do not see how a man under suspicion is to rebut such sinister scandals. The boys, with the help and encouragement of several members of the staff, made up a satirical play full of the puns and classical tags and ancient venerable turns of humour usual in such compositions, against this Barbarian invader and his new laboratories. It was the mock trial of an incendiary found trying to burn down the new laboratories. It was 'full of envenomed and insulting references' to all the new headmaster was supposed to hold dear. Finally it was rehearsed before him. He sat brooding over it thoughtfully, as shaft after shaft was launched against him. 'It didn't seem so funny then,' said my informant, 'as it had done when we prepared it.' It went to a 'ragged and unconvinced applause.' At the end 'came a pause—a stillness that could be felt.' The headmaster sat with downcast face, thinking.

I suppose he was chiefly busy reckoning how soon he would be rid of this hostile generation of elder boys. They had to go. It was a pity, but nothing was to be done with them. The school had to grow out of them, as it had to grow out of its disloyal staff.

He rose slowly in his seat. 'Boys, we will regard this as the final performance,' he said, and departed thoughtfully, making no further comment. He took no action in the matter, attempted neither reproof nor punishment. He dropped the matter with a magnificent contempt. And, says the old boy who tells the story, from that time the spirit of the school seemed to change in his favour. The old order had discharged its venom. The boys began to realise the true value of the forces of spite and indolent obstructiveness with which their youth was in alliance.

§ 4

Not always did Sanderson carry things off with an equal dignity.   His temperament was choleric, and ever and again his smouldering indignation at the obstinate folly and jealousy that hampered his work blazed out violently.   Dignified silence is impossible as a permanent pose for a teacher whose duty is to express and direct.   Sanderson's business was to get ideas into resisting heads; he was not a born orator but a confused, abundant speaker, and he had to scold, to thrust strange sayings at them, to force their inattention, to beat down an answering ridicule.   He was often simply and sincerely wrathful with them, and in his early years he thrashed a great deal.   He thrashed hard and clumsily in a white-heat of passion—'a hail of swishing strokes that seemed almost to envelop one.'   A newspaper or copybook at the normal centre of infliction availed but little. Cuts fell everywhere on back or legs or fingers. He had been sorely tried, he had been overtried. It was a sort of heartbreak of blows.

The boys argued mightily about these unorthodox swishings. It was all a part of Sanderson being a strange creature and not in the tradition. It was lucky no one was ever injured. But they found something in their own unregenerate natures that made them understand and sympathise with this eager, thwarted stranger and his thunderstorms of anger. Generally he was a genial person, and that, too, they recognised. It is manifest quite early in the story that Sanderson interested his boys as his predecessor had never done. They discussed his motives, his strange sayings, his peculiar locutions with accumulating curiosity. Two sorts of schoolmasters boys respect: those who are completely dignified and opaque to them, and those who are transparent enough to show honesty at the core. Sanderson was transparently honest. If he was not pompously dignified he was also extraordinarily free from vanity; and if he thrust work and toil upon his boys it was at any rate not to spare himself that he did so. And he won them also by his wonderful teaching. In the early days he did a lot of the science teaching himself; later on the school grew too big for him to do any of this.

All the old boys I have been able to consult agree that his class instruction was magnificent.

Every year in the history of Sanderson's head-mastership shows a growing understanding between the boys and himself. 'Beans,' they called him, but every year it was less and less necessary to 'Give 'm Beans,' as the vulgar say. The tale of storms and thrashings dwindles until it vanishes from the story. In the last decade of his rule there was hardly any corporal punishment at all. The whole school as time went on grew into a humorous affectionate appreciation of his genius. It was a sunny, humorous school when I knew it; there was little harshness and no dark corners. No boy had been expelled for a long time.

§ 5

The official life gives a diagram and particulars of the growth of the school during Sanderson's time, and there is no need to repeat those particulars here. From 1892 to 1900 there was no very remarkable increase in the number of boys; it rose from ninety-odd to a hundred and twenty or so. Then as Sanderson's grip became sure there followed a rapid expansion.

From 1900 onwards Oundle grew about as fast as it was possible to grow. New laboratories were built, new subjects introduced so as to furnish a wider and wider variety of courses to meet such intellectual types as the school had hitherto failed to interest. There was a great development of biological and agricultural work from about 1909 onward. The attention given to art increased, and there was a great change and revolution in the history teaching. By 1920 the numbers of the school were soaring up towards six hundred. He wanted them to go to eight hundred, because he still wanted to increase the variety of courses, and the larger numbers gave a better prospect of classifying out the boys effectively and making sure that each course of studies was sufficiently attended to keep it active and efficient.

The prestige of the school grew even more rapidly than its size. From 1905 onward the inquiring parent who wanted something more than school games and *esprit de corps* was sure to hear of Oundle.

And Sanderson was growing with his school.

Every installment of success stimulated him to new experiments and fresh innovations. No one learnt so much at Oundle as he did, and it is with that growth of his conception of school method and his widening vision of the schoolmaster's rôle in the world that we must now proceed to deal.

CHAPTER III

THE REPLACEMENT OF COMPETITION BY GROUP WORK

§ 1

WHEN Sanderson first came to Oundle his ideas seem to have differed from the normal scholastic opinion of his time mainly in his conviction of the interestingness and attractiveness of real scientific work for many types of boys that the established classical and stylistic mathematical teaching failed to grip. He developed these new aspects of school work, and his earliest success lay in the fact that he got a higher percentage of boys interested and active in school work than was usual elsewhere, and that the report of this and the report of his wholesome and stimulating personality spread into the world of anxious parents. But it early became evident to him that the new subjects necessitated methods of handling in vivid contrast to the methods stereotyped for the classical and mathematical courses.

There have been three chief phases in the history of educational method in the last five centuries, the phase of compulsion, the phase of competition, and the phase of natural interest. They overlap and mingle. Medieval teaching being largely in the hands of celibates, who had acquired no natural understanding of children and young people, and who found them extremely irritating, irksome, or exciting, was stupid and brutal in the extreme. Young people were driven along a straight and narrow road to a sort of prison of dusty knowledge by teachers almost as distressed as themselves. The medieval school went on to the chant of rote-learning with an accompaniment of blows, insults, and degradations of the dunce-cap type. The Jesuit schools, to which the British public schools owe so much, sought a human motive in vanity and competition; they turned to rewards, distinctions, and competitions. Sir Francis Bacon recommended them justly as the model schools of his time. The class-list with its pitiless relegation of two-thirds of the class to self-conscious mediocrity and dufferdom was the symbol of this second, slightly more enlightened phase. The school of the rod gave place to the school of the class-list. An aristocracy of leading boys made the pace and the rest of the school found its compensation in games or misbehaviour. So long as the sole subjects of instruction remained two dead languages and formal mathematics, subjects essentially unappetising to sanely constituted boys, there was little prospect of getting school method beyond this point.

By the end of the eighteenth century schoolmasters were beginning to realise what most mothers know by instinct, that there is in all young people a curiosity, a drive to know, an impulse to learn, that is available for educational ends, and has still to be properly exploited for educational ends. It is not within our present scope to discuss Pestalozzi, Froebel, and the other great pioneers in this third phase of education. Nearly all children can be keenly interested in some subject, and there are some subjects that appeal to nearly all children. Directly you cease to insist upon a particular type of achievement in a particular line of attainment, directly your school gets out of the narrow lane and moves across open pasture, it goes forward of its own accord. The class-list and the rod, so necessary in the dusty fury of the lane, cease to be necessary. In the effective realisation of this Sanderson was a leader.

For a time he let the classical and literary work of the school run on upon the old competition-compulsion, class-list lines. For some years he does not seem to have realised the possibility of changes in these fields. But from the first in his mechanical teaching and very soon in mathematics the work ceased to have the form of a line of boys all racing to acquire an identical parcel of knowledge, and took on the form more and more of clusters of boys surrounding an attractive problem. There grew up out of the school Science a periodic display, the Science Conversazione, in which groups of youngsters displayed experiments and collections they had co-operated to produce. Later on a Junior Conversazione developed. These conversaziones show the Oundle spirit in its most typical expression. Sanderson derived much from the zeal and interest these groups of boys displayed. He realised how much finer and how much more fruitful was the mutual stimulation of a common end than the vulgar effort for a class place. The clever boy under a class-list system loves the shirker and the dullard who make the running easy, but a group of boys working for a common end display little patience with shirking. The stimulus is much more intimate, and it grows. Jones minor is told to play up, exactly as he is told to play up in the playing field.

In the summer term the conversazione in its fully developed form took up a large part of the energy of the school. Says the official life:

'All the senior boys in the school were eligible for this work, the only qualification necessary being a willingness to work and to sacrifice some, at least, of one's free time. There was never any dearth of willing workers, the total number often exceeding two hundred. The chief divisions of the conversazione were: Physics and Mechanics; Chemistry; Biology; and Workshops. A boy who volunteered to help was left free to choose which branch he would adopt. Having chosen, he gave his name to the master in charge; if he had any particular experiment in view, he mentioned it, and if suitable, it was allotted to him. If he had no suggestion, an experiment was suggested, and he was told where information could be obtained.

As a general rule two or three boys worked together at any one experiment.

'Some of the experiments chosen required weeks of preparation; there was apparatus to be made and fitted up, information to be sought and absorbed, so that on the final day an intelligent account could be given to any visitor watching the experiment. This work was all done out of school hours. Four or five days before Speech Day, ordinary school lessons ceased for those taking part in the conversazione; the laboratories, class-rooms, and workshops were portioned out so that each boy knew exactly where he was to work, and how much space he had. The setting up of the experiments began. To any one visiting the school on these particular days it must have seemed in a state of utter confusion, boys wandering about in all directions apparently under no supervision, and often to all appearances with no purpose. A party might be met with a jam-jar and fishing-net near the river; others might be found miles away on bicycles, going to a place where some particular flower might be found. Three or four boys would appear to be smashing up an engine and scattering its parts in all directions, while others could be seen wheeling a barrow-load of bricks or trying to mix a hod of mortar. Gradually a certain amount of order appeared, some experiments were tried and found to work satisfactorily, others failed, and investigation into the cause of failure had to be carried out. As the final day approached excitement increased, frantic telegrams were sent to know, for example, if the liquid air had been despatched, frequent visits to the railway-station were made in the hopes of finding some parcel had arrived; sometimes it was even necessary to motor to Peterborough to pick up material which otherwise would arrive too late. A programme giving a short description of the experiment or exhibit had to pass through the printer's hands. At last everything would be ready; occasionally, but very seldom, an experiment had to be abandoned or another substituted at the last moment.'

The year 1905 marked a phase in the co-operative system of work on the mechanical side with the machining and erection of a six-horse-power reversing engine, designed for a marine engine of 3500 horse-power. Castings and drawings were supplied by the North Eastern Marine Engineering Works. The engine was a triumphant success, and thereafter a number of engines has been built by groups of boys. Concurrently with this steady replacement of the instructional-exercise system by the group-activity system, the mathematical work became less and less a series of exercises in style and more and more an attack upon problems needing solution in the workshops and laboratories, with the solution as the real incentive to the work. These dips into practical application gave a great stimulus to the formal mathematical teaching, for the boys realised as they could never have done otherwise the value of such work as a 'tool-sharpening' exercise of ultimately real value.

§ 2

Quite early in his Oundle days Sanderson displayed his disposition towards collective as against solitary activity in his dealings with the school music. When he came to the school the 'musical' boys were segregated from the non-musical in a choir; the rest listened in conscious exclusion and inferiority. But from the outset he set himself to make the whole school sing and attend to music. The few boys with bad ears were carried along with the general flood; the discord they made was lost in the mass effect. Towards the end a very great proportion of the boys were keen listeners to and acute critics of music. They would crowd into the Great Hall on Sunday evenings to listen to the organ recital with which that day usually concluded.

§ 3

Presently Sanderson began to apply the lessons he had learnt from grouping boys for scientific work to literature and history. Most of us can still recall the extraordinary dreariness of school literature teaching; the lesson that was a third-rate lecture, the note-taking, the rehearsal of silly opinions about books unread and authors unknown, the horrible annotated editions, the still more horrible text-books of literature. Sanderson set himself to sweep all this away. A play, he held, was primarily to be played, and the way to know and understand it was to play it. The boys must be cast for parts and learn about the other characters in relation to the one they had taken.

Questions of language and syntax, questions of interpretation, could be dealt with best in relation to the production. But most classes had far too many boys to be treated as a single theatrical company, so small groups of boys were cast for each part. There would be three or four Othellos, three or four Desdemonas or Iagos. They would act their parts simultaneously or successively. The thing might or might not ripen into a chosen cast giving a costume performance in public. The important thing is that the boys were brought into the most active contact possible with the reality of the work they studied. The groups discussed stage 'business' and gesture and the precise stress to lay on this or that phrase. The master stood like a producer in the auditorium of the Great Hall. Let any one compare the vitality of that sort of thing with the ordinary lesson from an annotated text-book.

The group system was extended with increasing effectiveness into more and more of the literary and historical work. Here the School Library took the place of the laboratory and was indeed as necessary to the effective development of the group method. The official life of Sanderson gives a typical scheme of operations pursued in the case of a form studying the period 1783–1905. The subject was first divided up into parts, such as the state of affairs preceding the French Revolution; the French Revolution in relation to England; the industrial system and economic problems generally; and so on. The form divided up into groups and each group selected a part or a section of a part for its study. The objective of each group was the preparation of a report, illustrated by maps, schedules, and so forth, upon the section it had studied. After a preliminary survey of the whole field under the direction of a master, each boy followed up the particular matter assigned to him by individual reading for a term, supplemented when necessary by consultation with the master. Then came the preparation of maps and other material, the assembling of illuminating quotations from the books studied, the drafting of the group's report, the discussion of the report. In some cases where the group was in disagreement there would be a minority report.

In this way there was scarcely a boy in the form who did not feel himself contributing and necessary to the general result, and who was not called upon not merely by his master but by his colleagues, for some special exertion. It might be thought that the departmentalising of the subject among groups would mean that the knowledge would accumulate in pockets, but this was not the case. Boys of separate groups talked with one another of their work and found a lively interest in their different points of view. It is rare that boys who have received the same lesson can find much in it to talk about, unless it is a comparison of who has retained most, but a boy who has been preparing maps of the Napoleonic military campaigns may find the liveliest interest in another who has been following the history of the same period from the point of view of sea power. There was indeed a very considerable amount of interchange, and when it came to facing external examiners and testing the general knowledge attained, the Oundle boys were found to compare favourably with boys who had been drummed in troops through complete histories of the chosen period.

This group system of work had arisen naturally out of the conditions of the new laboratory teaching, and it had been developed for the sake of its educational effectiveness; but as it grew it became more and more evident to Sanderson that its effects went far beyond mere intellectual attainment. It marked a profound change in the spirit of the school. It was not only that the spirit of co-operation had come in. That had already been present on the cricket and football fields. But the boys were working to make something or to state something and not to gain something. It was the spirit of creation that now pervaded the school.

And he perceived, too, that the boys he would now be sending out into the world must needs carry that creative spirit with them and play a very different part from the ambitious star boys who went on from a training under the older methods. They would play an as yet incalculable part in redeeming the world from the wild orgy of competition that was now afflicting it. In one of his very characteristic sermons he gave his ripened conception of this side of his work. He had been speaking, perhaps with a certain idealisation, of the old craftsmen's guilds—with a glance or so at the Grocers' Company. The school, he declared, was to be no longer an arena but a guild. For what was a guild?

'A community of co-workers and no competition, that was its idea. It is all based on the system of apprenticeships and co-workers. The apprentices helped the masters in every way they could; even the masters were grouped together for mutual assistance and were called assistants. The Company was a mystery or guild of craftsmen and dealers, and their aim was to produce good craftsmen and good dealers.

'To-day, in these days of renascence, we return to the aim and methods of the guilds. Boys are to be apprentices and master-workers and co-workers. In a community this needs must be. We are called to a definite work, all who are privileged to attend here, staff and boys alike—the work of infusing life into the boys committed to our care. Nor can any one stand out of this and seek work elsewhere. Nemesis sets in for all who try to live for themselves alone. They may try to work—but their work is sterile. The community calls for the energies and activities of all. We are beginning to learn something of what this means. It does not mean an abandonment of the best methods of the past. But it does mean that we have to concern ourselves with the pressing needs and problems of to-day, and join in the work. I do not dwell on this now. My mind goes off to the possible effect of these ideas on the general life of the school.

'The working of these ideas is well seen already in the outdoor life of the school. We see it when houses are getting their teams together to join a competition for a shield, say. We see the mutual help, the voluntary practice, the consultations of the captain with others. We see it in the work in the Cadet Corps. We see it in the preparation for a play—this time, the *Midsummer Night's Dream*. We see it in the new work in the library, and we see it as clearly as in anything in the preparation for a conversazione. No more valuable training can be given than this last—well worth all the many kinds of sacrifice it entails. From it, at any rate, the spirit of competition is, I think, altogether removed. Boys, we believe, set forth to do their work as well as they possibly can— but not to beat one another . . . I dwell upon these things because we hope that all boys will become workers at last, with interest and zeal, in some part of the field of creation and inquiry, which is the true life of the world. It is from such workers, investigators, searchers, the soul of the nation is drawn. We will first of all transform the life of the school, then the boys, grown into men—and girls from their schools grown into women—whom their schools have enlisted into this service, will transform the life of the nation and of the whole world.'

CHAPTER IV

THE RE-ESTABLISHMENT OF RELATIONS BETWEEN SCHOOL AND REALITY

§ 1

IN the previous chapter I have told how Sanderson was taught by his laboratories and library the possibility of a new type of school with a new spirit, and how he grew to realise that an organisation of such new schools, a multiplication of Oundles, must necessarily produce a new spirit in social and industrial life. Concurrently with that, the obvious implications of applied science were also directing his mind to the close reaction between schools and the organisation of the economic life of the community.

It is amusing to reflect that Sanderson probably owed his appointment at Oundle to the simple desire of various members of the Grocers' Company for a good school of technical science. They did not want any change in themselves, they did not want any change in the world nor in the methods of trading and employment, but they did want to see their sons and directors and managers equipped with the sharper, more modern edge of a technical scientific training. Germany had frightened them. If this new training could be technical without science and modern without liberality, so much the better. So the business man brought his ideas to bear upon Oundle, to produce quite beyond his expectation a counter-offensive of the school upon business organisation and methods. Oundle built its engines, organised itself as an efficient munitions factory during the war, made useful chemical inquiries, extended its work into agriculture, analysed soils and manures for the farmers of its district, ran a farm and did much able competent technical work, but it also set itself to find out what were the aims and processes of business and what were the reactions of these processes upon the life of the community. From the laboratory a boy would go to a careful examination of labour conditions under the light of Ruskin's *Unto This Last;* he was brought to a balanced and discriminating attitude towards strikes and lock-outs; he was constantly reminded

that the end of industry is not profits but life—
a more abundant life for men.

As one reads through the sermons and addresses
that are given in *Sanderson of Oundle* one finds
a steadily growing consciousness of the fact that
there was a considerable and increasing proportion of Oundle boys destined to become masters,
managers, and leaders in industrial and business
life, and with that growing consciousness there is
a growing determination that the school work
they do shall be something very far beyond the
acquisition of money-getting dodges and devices
and commercialised views of science. More and
more does he see the school not as a training
ground of smart men for the world that is, but as
a preliminary working model of the world that
is to be.

Two quotations from two of Sanderson's sermons will serve to mark how vigorously he is
tugging back the English schools from the gentle-
manly aloofness of scholarship and school-games
to a real relationship to the current disorder of
life, and how high he meant to carry them to
dominance over that disorder.

The first extract is from a sermon on Faraday.

Under Sanderson, it has been remarked, Faraday ousted St. Anthony from being the patron saint of Oundle School. 'With what abundant prodigality,' Sanderson exclaims, 'has Nature given up of her secrets since his day!'

'A hundred years ago Man and Nature as we think of them to-day were unexplored by science; to-day a new world, a new creation. Industrial life has developed, machinery, discoveries, inventions—steam engine, gas engine, dynamo—electrical machinery, telegraphy, radioactive bodies, tremendous openings out of chemistry, biology, economics, ethics. All new. These are Thy works, O God, and tell of Thee. Not now only may we search for Thy Presence in the places where Thou wert wont in days of old to come to man. Not there only. Not only now in the stars of heaven; or by the seashore, or in the waters of the river, or of the springs; among the trees, the flowers, the corn and wine, on the mountain or in the plain; not now only dost Thou come to man in Thy works of art, in music, in literature; but Thou, O God, dost reveal Thyself in all the multitude of Thy works; in the workshop, the factory, the mine, the laboratory, in industrial life. No symbolism here, but the Divine God. A new Muse is here—

> 'Mightier than Egypt's tombs,
> Fairer than Grecia's, Roma's temples.
> Prouder than Milan's statued, spired cathedral,
> More picturesque than Rhenish castle-keeps,
> We plan even now to raise, beyond them all,
> Thy great cathedral, sacred industry, no tomb—
> A keep for Life.'

And the builders, a mighty host of men: Homeric heroes, fighting against a foe, and yet not a foe, but an invisible, impalpable thing wherein the combatant is the shadow of the assailant.

'Mighty men of science and mighty deeds. A Newton who binds the universe together in uniform law; Lagrange, Laplace, Leibnitz with their wondrous mathematical harmonies; Coulomb measuring out electricity; Oversted with the brilliant flash of insight "that the electric conflict acts in a revolving manner"; Faraday, Ohm, Ampère, Joule, Maxwell, Hertz, Röntgen; and in another branch of science, Cavendish, Davy, Dalton, Dewar; and in another, Darwin, Mendel, Pasteur, Lister, Sir Ronald Ross. All these and many others, and some whose names have no memorial, form a great host of heroes, an army of soldiers—fit companions of those of whom the poets have sung; all, we may be sure, living daily in the presence of God, bending like the reed before His will; fit companions of the knights of old of whom the poets sing, fit companions of the men whose names are renowned in history, fit companions of the great statesmen and warriors whose names resound through the world.

'There is the great Newton at the head of this list comparing himself to a child playing on the seashore gathering pebbles, whilst he could see with prophetic vision the immense ocean of truth yet unexplored before him. At the end is the discoverer Sir Ronald Ross, who had gone out to India in the medical service of the Army, and employed his leisure in investigating the ravishing diseases which had laid India low and stemmed its development. In twenty years of labour he discovers how malaria is transmitted and brings the disease within the hold of man.'

The second is from a sermon called 'The Garden of Life.'

'As Canon Driver says, "Man is not made simply to enjoy life; his end is not pleasure; nor are the things he has to do necessarily to give pleasure or lead to what men call happiness." This is not the biological purpose of man. His purpose or instinctive end is to develop the capacities of the garden in the wilderness of nature; to adapt it to his own ends, *i.e.* to the ends of the races of men. Or, as we would now say, his aim is to take his part in the making of his kind; and he is to "keep it," or guard it—*i.e.* he is to conquer the jungle in it, to prevent it from roving wild again, from reverting to the jungle, from losing law and order, from becoming unruly and disorderly, from breaking loose and running amok. He is to bring and maintain order out of the tangle of things, he is to diagnose diseases; he is to co-ordinate the forces of nature; he is above all things to reveal the spirit of God in all the works of God.

'And in all this we read the duty and service of schools. The business of schools is through and by the use of a common service to get at the true spiritual nature of the ordinary things we have to deal with. The spirit of the true active life does not come to us *only* in those experiences we have been so accustomed to think of as beautiful and revealing. The active spirit of life is not revealed simply by the arts—the beautiful

arts as they may be thought—of music or painting, or literature. These indeed may be only and
abundantly *material*, and the eye and ear may be
blind and deaf to the active, creative, discovering,
revealing spirit. "Painting, or art generally, as
such," says Ruskin in his *Modern Painters*, "with
all its technicalities, difficulties, executive skills,
pleasant and agreeable sensations, and its particular ends, is nothing but an expressive language, invaluable if we know it as we might know
it as the vehicle of thought, but by itself nothing."
He who has learnt what is commonly considered
as the whole art of painting, that is the art of
representing any natural object faithfully, has as
yet only learnt the language by which his thoughts
are to be expressed. One language or mode of
expression may be more difficult than another;
but it is not by the mode of representing and
saying, but by the greatness, the awakening, the
transmuting and transfiguring conception and
knowledge of the thought presented, that the gift
cometh, that man is created. Awkward, dis-
cordant, stammering attempts may be the burning
message of a new hope. But this "voice" of art
is too often drowned. It is drowned by executive

skill—as is the history of all art—when this skill stretches itself to present things that are static, motionless, dead. . . .

'It is especially our duty to reveal the spirit of God in the things of science and of the practical life. Herein lies a new revelation, a new language, a direct symbolism. Science, just like art and music, can be materialistic—science can aim only at mechanical advancement and worldly wealth, which is not wealth at all—just as art can aim only at pleasure, desire, and drawing-room appreciation. But this need not be so. Certainly no one in a responsible position can teach science for long without the coming of the revelation of a new voice, a new method of expression, a new art—revealing quite changed standards of value, quite new significances of what we speak of as culture, beauty, love, justice. A new voice speaks to the souls of men and women calling for a new age with all its altered relationships and adventures of life.

'With eyes opened to this new art you can wander through the science block and find in it all a new Bible, a new book of Genesis. So we believe. This is our duty and our faith. Into this Paradise have you been placed to dress it and to keep it.'

Let me turn from these two passages of talk to his boys—they are rescued from a mass of pencil notes in his study—to a passage from an address delivered in the Great Hall in Leeds in 1920. It shows very plainly the quality of his conception of what I have called the return of schools to reality.

'Schools should be miniature copies of the world. We often find that methods adopted in school are just the methods we should like applied in the state. We should, in fact, direct school life so that the spirit of it may be the spirit which will tend to alleviate social and industrial conditions. I will give an example of the kind of influence the ideals and methods of a school can exert upon the working life. I will take a condition of labour which is now recognised as probably the greatest of tragedies. It is the slow decay of the faculties of crowds of men and women, caused by the nature of their employment—the tragedy of the unstretched faculties. So common is it, and ordinary, that we pass it by on one side; but no one can go into a factory without seeing workers engaged in work which is far below their capacities.

Decay sets in, and the death of talent and enthusiasm, the inspirer of creative work. A little
thought will convince us that the process of decay
of such a delicate and vital organism as the brain
is bound to set up violent, destructive, anarchic
forces which go on for several years. A recent
writer in the *Times Educational Supplement* (and
this paper cannot be called revolutionary) says
that the tragedy of undeveloped talent is being
seen more and more to be a gigantic waste of
potentiality and an unpardonable cruelty. It is
a tragic disease and produces in early life startling
intellectual and moral disturbances, which are
the natural sources of unrest. As years go on a
mental stupor sets in, and there is peace, but peace
on a low plane of life. The loss to the community
by this waste is colossal, and it is not too much
to say that the output of man could be multiplied
beyond conception.

'Schools should send boys out into the industrial world whose aim should be to study these
tragedies, and by experiments, by new inventions,
by organisation, try, we may hope, by some of
their own school experience, to alleviate the disease. To my mind this is the supreme aim of
schools in the new era.'

CHAPTER V

THE GROWTH OF SANDERSON SHOWN IN HIS SERMONS AND SCRIPTURE LESSONS

§ 1

BEFORE I go on to a discussion of the latest, broadest, and most interesting phase of Sanderson's mental life, I would like to give my readers as vivid a picture as I can of his personality and his methods of delivery. I have tried to convey an impression of his stout and ruddy presence, his glancing spectacles, his short, compact but allusive delivery, his general personal jolliness. I will give now a sketch of one of his Scripture lessons made by two of the boys in the school. Nothing I think could convey so well his rich discursiveness nor the affectionate humour he inspired throughout the school. Here it is.

'SCRIPTURE LESSON

'*Delivered by F. W. Sanderson on Sunday, 25th May 1919, and taken down word for word by X and Y, and subsequently written up by them.*

'*Limitations of space and time have prevented them from including all the lesson. Omissions have been indicated. They apologise for the lapses of the speaker into inaudibility, which were not their fault. They do not hold themselves in any way responsible for the opinions expressed herein.*

'ANALYSIS

'of the portions copied.

'Characteristic portions in the Gospel of St. Matthew.

'Obstinacy of the Oxford and Cambridge Schools Examination Board.

'Character of the devil, according to some modern writers.

'First act of our Lord on beginning the Galilean Ministry.

'Empire Day.

'*Subject of the Scripture lesson:*—*St. Matthew, chaps. iv and v.*

('The Temptations, the commencement of the Galilean Ministry, the first portion of the Sermon on the Mount.')

'(The headmaster enters, worries his gown, sits down, adjusts his waistcoat, and coughs once.)

'The—um—er—I am taking you through the Gospel of St. Matthew. I think, as a matter of fact, we got to the end of the third chapter. We won't spend much time over the fourth. The fourth, I think, is the—er—er—Temptations, which I have already taken with you—a rather— er—very interesting—ah—very interesting—er— survival. That the Temptation Narrative should have survived shows that there is probably something of value in it or I do not think it would have survived. There are two incidents of very similar character of—er—very—er—similar character and—ah—different to a certain extent from everything else—er—ah— There is a boy in that corner not listening to me. Who is that boy in the corner there? No, not you—two rows in front. I will come down to you later, my boy. There are two incidents in the Gospel Narrative which are similar in—er—character and which I have for the moment called "Survivals"—very characteristic, namely, the somewhat surprising narrative of the Temptation of our Lord, and the other the account of the Transfiguration. These are different in form and character from other narratives, just in the same way as the account of our Lord sending messages to the Baptist differs from others. Er—yes—that last one. I should put them together as coming from a similar source (lapse into inaudibility—bow wow wow. Unique in characteristic—bow wow wow—Somewhat subtle—bow wow). One remarks that the Temptations are always looked at from the personal point of view, which I have put down in my synopsis. Has anybody here got my synopsis? lend it to me a moment. I don't think the personal significance of the Gospel stories has importance nowadays. We needn't consider it. That's what I think about things in general. Personal importance giving place to universal needs. We are not so much concerned with whether boys do *evil* or not. Of course it annoys me if I find a boy doing evil. Leading others astray. Shockingly annoying. Oughtn't to be. Like continuous mathematics not enabling a boy to pass in arithmetic—bow wow wow—screw loose. See what I mean, K——? Not referring to you, my boy (laughter). Hunt me up something in Plato about all these things. During the last generation—

'(Half a page omitted.)

'Just in the same way from another point of view shall we live for own advancement, which we are continually tempted to do? It's awfully annoying if you do certain things and people won't recognise them. I was pretty heftily annoyed myself at a meeting of the Oxford and Cambridge Board. Professor Barker—great man —I nearly always agree with him. Professor Barker. They had made science compulsory for the school certificate. Bow wow wow. I don't want boys turned aside from their main purpose to have to get up scraps and snippets of science. Literary pursuits and so on. I wouldn't have it at any price. Bow wow wow. Modern languages are compulsory too. By looking at a boy's French set I can tell whether he can pass or not. Bow wow. Professor Barker proposed that science should be voluntary. I seconded him, but I said that languages should be voluntary as well. He didn't see that at all. Isn't it enough to make a man angry?

'(Half a dozen lines omitted from our note as incomprehensible.)

'Now I am inclined to think that Satan in this Gospel is not intended to be the Satan of our minds—the prince of evil. He is intended to be more like the Satan in the book of Job. He is the devil's advocate. He argues for the other side. For the opposition. He is put up to create opposition. This may in itself be a valuable thing. I don't know that I need go further into it. I would just like to tell you this, boys. Some modern writers, especially Bernard Shaw, have a very high esteem for the devil. He[1] prefers hell to heaven. So he says. Of course he hasn't been there, so he can't tell. So he is voted a dangerous personage because, dear souls, they don't know what he means. What *he* means is that heaven as it has been run down to and God as He has been run down to—everything placid and simple and inactive and non-creative and sleepy. People don't worship God. They worship (burble burble). They don't disturb their minds and think about things. That's what he means. Yes. Man and Superman. Activity of intellect. That's

---

[1] Mr. Shaw.

more or less what he has in mind. He prefers people doing something outrageously wrong than doing nothing at all. I don't know if it's true; it's all expressed in Greek thought.

'(Four pages omitted on running with the tide, Lloyd George, the importance of French in examinations, and the correct way of getting a true national spirit.)

'Well, our Lord now proceeded to found His Galilean Ministry. And what was the first thing He did, L——? It's quite obvious. What did He do? Obvious. Were you thinking of what I said just now? No, sir. My stream of words goes over you, not through you. Obvious. Now what was the first thing He did? What is obviously the first thing He did? Why, it's painfully obvious, even to L——. What was it? What? Where are we, L——? L—— has lost the place. Which paragraph do I mean, L——? Read the paragraph I mean. No. I have finished that. Next one. Obvious. What is it about? Yes, what is it about? What is it about? Two or four? Yes, four! Now what is obvious? Obvious! Now you've just got it, and you're ten minutes behind. Of course. The first obvious

thing He had to do was to get a band of faithful
disciples. Very first thing He did. What did
He call them to be? To be what? Fishers of
Men. Obvious.

'(Five pages omitted on Empire Day, Medical
Study, and Cancer.)

'Now the—er—the Sermon on the Mount.
You have heard this ever since you were on your
mother's knee. At least I hope so. Beyond the
historical times of your memory. For you, the
Sermon on the Mount is as old as the ages. And
yet I dare trespass on the Sermon on the Mount.
"I've heard of it before," you say. "I'm tired of
it. Do something fresh." Boys, you must go and
read old things and breathe into them the new
Spirit of Life. Now what is that chapter in
Ezekiel, boys? Do you know the number of the
page, and the paragraph, and the chapter? No.
What am I talking about? Why, the valley of
dry bones. Never heard of it! No. Is it in
Jeremiah, Ezekiel, or where, or Habakkuk? Is
it in Ezekiel 1? No. 36? No. 37? Yes. Dry
Bones. Bones. Yes. That's what. I am going
to take you to a valley of dry bones. Dry Bones.
Bones. It is your business to go into the dry

bones of the past and cover them with flesh, and breathe into them the new Spirit. I often read the Sermon on the Mount. It never bores me. I have more excuse to be bored than you. I learned it, gracious goodness, how long ago! Beyond Historic times. I loved it as a boy. Dry Bones.

'(Three pages on the Sermon on the Mount.)

'Now yesterday was Empire Day. Why did you want me to put the flag up? Rule Britannia! Britannia rules the waves! Is not that it? (Yes, sir.) Dear boys! I wouldn't throw cold water on it for worlds. Well, you had your flag. It didn't fly. There was no wind behind it. There was no devil to blow it. Dear boys, you wanted that flag for a reason I think a shade wrong. It wouldn't be within the—what's the word I want? —suited for our modern gauges. The new world won't come until we give up the idea of Conquest and Extension of Empire—no new kingdom until its members are imbued with the principles that competition is wrong, that conquest is wrong, that co-operativeness is right, and sacrifice a law of nature. Now, how do the seven Beatitudes read with *Rule Britannia?* Now you say you believe

in your Bibles. You say you are Christians.
Pious Christians. You would be most annoyed
if I called you heathens. Well, if so, you believe
that these are right:—

'Blessed are the poor in spirit, for theirs is the
kingdom of heaven. Rule Britannia!

'Blessed are they that mourn, for they shall be
comforted. Rule Britannia!

'Blessed are the meek, for they shall inherit the
earth. Rule Britannia!

'Blessed are they that hunger and thirst after
righteousness, for they shall be filled. Britannia
rules the waves!

'Blessed are the merciful, for they shall obtain
mercy. Rule Britannia!

'Blessed are the pure in heart, for they shall
see all that is worth seeing and living for. Wave
your flag! Rule Britannia!

'Blessed are the peacemakers, for they shall be
called sons of God. Rule Britannia!

'Blessed are they that have been persecuted for
righteousness sake. Rule Britannia! It is in-
congruous. . . .

'Dear souls! My dear souls! I wouldn't lead
you astray for anything. I can't explain it . . .

this national spirit of yours.   Beneath it all there is a spirit of great righteousness.   I wouldn't tamper with it for thousands of pounds.   But you must just see the other side. . . .

   '(Starts on the Salt of the Earth, but is interrupted by time.   Sets a heavy prep., and goes.)'

§ 2

Now that was the key in which Sanderson dealt with his boys and in which he gave his message to the world.   And that is also the key in which they dealt with him.   I want to clear out of the reader's mind any idea that this great teacher of men was a solemn and superior person, clear, exact, and exalted, and that his boys had any vague sentimental worship for him.   They laughed at him, loved him, understood him, assimilated his ideas, and worked with him.   He was much more like a sweating, panting, burly leader pushing a way for himself and others through a thorny thicket.   And when I sat in his study and read over the notes of his sermons and scripture lessons I got the same impression of a sturdy fighter thrusting through a tangle.

Altogether there were several hundred of these sermon-memoranda. He would take a quire of manuscript paper and write down his notes, not headings merely but sentences, writing very fast, missing out halves of words, leaving phrases incomplete. The result would be a little book with perhaps a title and a date scribbled on the back page. The dozen specimen sermons in the official Life were mostly taken from these rough drafts. There was also a quantity of printed sermons dating from his earliest days at Oundle. So that it was possible to trace his development from the days when every heretical utterance was jealously noted, to the days of complete freedom of thought and expression.

He came into the interlaced briars and brakes of modern religious thought, a trained theological student, but already a very broad one, far from the trite materialistic superstitions of the narrowly orthodox. 'Of what is termed "definite religious teaching" his boys received little,' says one of his clerical assistants. 'The Head fought shy of anything which he felt might cramp a boy's tendency to think for himself and develop his own views.'

This is far from the old days of salvation by belief.

He took Christ as the central figure in his teaching. In his early days he had prepared a parallel arrangement of the gospels, and this developed into his *Synopsis of the Life of Christ*. He seems to have clung stoutly to the authenticity of the recorded sayings of Christ, but he held himself free to doubt whether we have as yet 'got to the bottom of many sayings of the Master.' And, says the same witness, at once rather vaguely and rather illuminatingly: 'He brushed aside impatiently doubts as to the feasibility of this miracle or that. To any who seemed to be worrying about the actual turning of water into wine at Cana he would urge that they were missing the whole point; cold, lifeless water was turned into warm, life-giving wine—and this was the work of the Master and His new teaching. Could they doubt that? He seemed to feel acutely that the passing of the centuries is liable to bring a distortion as well as an enrichment of the Christian revelation, and for that reason he was always trying to meditate himself, and to get others to meditate, on the true characteristics of the Master in the earliest

The head among the parents

portraits of Him handed down to us in the Gospels.'

Like all religious teachers he emphasised some aspects of the general doctrine in preference to others, but his accent was never on the sacramental or ceremonial side. The root ideas of orthodox Christianity, the ideas of sin and an atonement, never very prominent in his teaching, faded more and more from his discourses as the years went on. He never seems to have had much sense of sin, and he laid an increasing stress on action, on courage and experiment. One saying he repeated endlessly, 'Give, and it shall be given unto you; good measure, pressed down, shaken together, running over, shall men give into your bosom.' Still more frequently he quoted, 'I came that ye might have life, and that ye might have it more abundantly.' In his later days that had become a new motto for Oundle School; it ousted 'God grant Grace' from the boys' thoughts in much the same way that Faraday for all spiritual purposes ousted St. Anthony as the patron saint of the school. And in the later sermons one would find side by side with Gospel sayings, exhortations from quite another quarter. The boys were

told to 'live dangerously.'   The Christ of later
Oundle became indeed a very Nietzschean Christ.

§ 3

Orthodox Christianity is built upon the doctrine
of the Fall of Man and the damnation of mankind, but I could find only the rarest and remotest
allusions to this ground beneath the Christian
corner-stone of salvation in the bale of sermons I
examined.   There is no evidence that Sanderson
ever denied the fallen state of man, but he never
alluded to it, and the general effect of his teaching
went far beyond a mere avoidance.   As his teaching developed, another word, a word infrequent in
the gospels, became dominant, the word 'creative.'
For any mention of 'salvation' you will find
twenty repetitions of 'creative.'   So far as I can
gather he took the word from a hitherto unrecog-
nised Christian father, St. Bertrand Russell.   And
I should submit the following passage from a
sermon on The Garden of Life, to any competent
theological body with very grave doubts whether
they would accept it as consistent with the teaching of any recognised Christian Church.

'God had created man, and had moulded and fashioned him, and had breathed into his nostrils the breath of life, and man became a living soul, possessed of the divine and eternal indestructible spirit, the God-like spirit which would fill him with the glorious and life-giving spirit of unrest, of unsatisfied longings and desire, of the instinctive natural urge to have more of life. A mighty power, a dynamic creative force, a daemonic increasing urge—against which the forces of hell, of destructiveness, of caprice, of lawlessness, of the jungle, cannot prevail. Under this power man and the races of man progress: but without this mental fight, this constant struggle, no life can come. I dwelt on this fact last time I spoke to you, having in mind the mental or intellectual aspect of it, especially for those of you who are working for some searching examinations: for without a persistent, painful, and often enough disappointing effort the understanding of things will not come to you, or to any of us.

'Be true to yourselves, suffer no artifice, or artificial understanding, to throw dust in your eyes. Do not struggle for a static victory. Be true to yourselves. Do not struggle for your own recognition, as it were, or for the mere appearance of knowledge—rather struggle to enter into the kingdom, the kingdom of service.

'And where can you find the inspiration and urge of life? The source is wonderfully drawn out for us in the illuminating and suggestive commentary on Genesis you have the advantage to study. A great human book is Canon Driver's *Commentary*, digging out for us the deep truths of life embedded in the ancient myths of Genesis. A study in the use of words; of what we can learn from words; a new form of text-book. Such a text-book as we should have for the new era. This picture of the coming and making of man tells us a story of the widest applicability. It is found in all the works of God; it is found in all our surroundings; it is found in all our work and toil; it is found most fully and actively in all our daily working life. God, we are told, made a garden for man, and there He placed him and gave him charge of it; and there the Lord God came and walked with man, and communed with man, and breathed into his nostrils the breath of life. And there He gave him his chief aim of life, his one purpose. And the Lord God took man, and put him in the Garden of Eden, to dress it and to keep it. And then with the memory and order of that garden in his mind He permitted him to receive knowledge, and then sent him out into the great wilderness to find his garden there.'

And here is another passage from a sermon entitled 'Creative.'

'In the beginning God created the heaven and the earth, and the earth was waste and void. The world was in chaos, darkness, and gloom. But it was not to be left in this state. All this condition of anarchy, this waste and void, was the material out of which a new world was to be created. Confused and impossible though everything appeared, yet there was something present that made steadfastly and incessantly for order. So we believe it is now, in the present state of things. All the conflicts and strifes of to-day are the breaking up of the fallow ground. They are the effort to create life. They are the messengers of the coming of the Son of Man. In storm and tempest cometh the Son of Man. Over all this lawless, shapeless, impossible material of chaos there brooded, we are told, the Spirit of God. The Spirit of God was brooding over the waters like a bird over its nest, and in due time, in the order of creation, a new life was to take shape, and a new world was to rise up. In stately, ordered, majestic manner with all the certainty and irresistible power of gravitation, step by step, stage by stage, out of the welter of anarchy, a life—a new life—was to come into the world. A new life came.

'And at each stage we hear the words of the Lord God, "Let there be," and "there was." And then: "God saw that it was good." There was evening, and there was morning—darkness changed into light—and the day's work was done. And God saw that it was good.

'So, too, it is and will be in the history of the human race. The uplifting of mankind, the coming of fuller life to nations, to man, to classes and sections of men, has come in epochs of change. Such stages in history are like the stages in the life history of a plant. There seem to be resting phases, epochs of apparent quiescence, the cessation of struggle.

'The fact is that some new freedom, some new principle of life, some desire to grow, has for a long time been taking root in the minds and souls of men. The urge to become more creative—to

gain more of life and give more of life—becomes
at last intense.   And there is an immense desire
to satisfy the great urge of nature.   The old order
passes.   The gathered forces seek release.   The
pangs of birth are upon us.'

The further one goes with Sanderson, the
stronger is one's sense of new wine fermenting in
the old bottle of orthodox Christian formulæ.   In
one of the late sermons he deliberately sets aside
the Epistles of the New Testament as of less
account than the gospels.   He was still diverging
when he died.   In the last year or so of his life
a new word crept into his talk and played an
increasingly important part in it.   That word was
'syncretism.'   He spoke of it more and more
plainly as an evil thing.   And I cannot but believe, knowing his sources of knowledge and the
angle at which he approached history, that he
must have been aware that doctrinal Christianity
—as detached from the personal teaching of Jesus
—is, with its Mithraic blood sacrifice and Sab-
bath keeping, its Alexandrine trinity, its Egyptian
priests, shaven and celibate, its Stella Maris and
infant Horus, the completest example of a syncretic religion in the world.   My impression is

that if he had lived another two years he would have shed his last vestiges of theological paraphernalia and gone straight back to the teaching of the Nazarene, openly and plainly. And that would have created a very embarrassing situation for the members of the Grocers' Company, in the school at Oundle.

§ 4

And what creed was taking the place of the old theological tangle? What interpretation was Sanderson putting upon this ever-new teaching of Christ in the world, that he was stripping so steadily out of its irrelevant casings of dogma and superstition? I cannot do better in answer to that than quote from one of his latest sermons, a sermon delivered on the reassembly of the school at the opening of a new school year.

'The fundamental instinct of life is to create, to make, to discover, to grow, to progress. Every one in some form or other has experience of this joy of creating; the joy of seeing the growth, the building, the change, the coming. The instinct of those in authority has recognised—without perhaps knowing it—the love to create, when they devised punishment—the treadmill, prisons, routine, all thwarting that free creative impulse to the point of torture. Or on a minor scale the trivial school stupidities and idlenesses of 'lines'; detentions without labour or sacrifice or both; or even the cheap and easy physical punishment. Such punishment, if not all inflicted punishment, springs out of the distinctive protective aim of slavery. Creative life comes slowly.

'Life, this beautiful, creative life, comes slowly through the ages, but it comes. Slowly mankind is emerging out of slavery into the beautiful freedom of creative life. Slowly mankind is realising the natural desire, the instinctive natural urge, the essential need for life—of each individual to be free. Free—*i.e.* free to strive, to endeavour, to reach onwards, to create, to make, to beget. The economic freedom of the individual has been slowly escaping throughout history. It burst into a new vigorous life through the hammering blows of the French Revolution. During the last century or more this principle of freedom has been changing our political relationships and values. This economic escape may be said to have reacted on science, and the modern developments of evolution have benefited by the spreading change in the temper of mind, and by the influx of workers and creative thinkers from the enslaved order.

'And this raises a large question which I have in mind this morning. Every one can see to-day the immensity of the problems before the world. It does not need much reflection, or foresight, or knowledge, to see that the organisation of the intercourse of races is hurrying on to becoming a dangerous problem. As has been said, and as any one I think with powers of sight can see, it is in a large sense a race between education and catastrophe. And the question we in schools have to ask is, Can we in schools be outside all this? Can we confine our work, our play, our necessary work, our necessary play, to the recognised, traditional work or play of schools? We here think not. We believe that schools should move on towards becoming always a microcosm of the new world. A microcosm, and experiment, of the standards of value, of the commandments, the statutes and judgments, of the organisation, of the visions and aims of a coming world. We must not get into our heads that these are theoretical things, it may be pure idealistic sort of things, or, it may be new and dangerous things. They are none of these things—they can be expressed in very everyday, homely, matter-of-fact things and in the doing of our ordinary work. Of course they do mean thought, a tendency to believe, a faith in boys—and they do mean labour, and sacrifice—as they are called or thought of at first—until both pass on into the beautiful life.

'Such aims and urges become terrific powers for prolonging the life of man; and as the stream of life goes on it becomes more and more like a vast river moving slowly forward with great power, receiving more and more of tributaries, slowly, strongly, surely flowing on "unto the estuary that enlarges, and spreads itself grandly as it pours its waters into the great ocean of sea."

'But the beginnings are here: and here boys must find themselves in the great stream of true life. They must find themselves in the land of the great vision, of faith, of service. No beating or marking of time here. No easy static state. No satisfaction with conventional static comfort. Here they will join in this great world-life. They came from their homes to join the great world-life here. Even these tiny boys here will feel that something is before them that matters, something of true life and true intent. They will get the germs of life from some of those things we are perpetually trying to do, and never succeeding in doing. They will catch the contagion of effort. For learning is not our object here, but doing. They may learn things in a deadly static way, they may learn much in a static way and gain nothing of life. Not here, I hope. No, the germs of life come from the spirit; from the incessant travail of the soul; from high intent; they come from the burning desire to know of the things that are coming into the world. . . .'

CHAPTER VI

THE WAR AND SANDERSON'S
PROPAGANDA OF RECONSTRUCTION

§ 1

THE disaster of the great war came to
Sanderson as a tremendous distressful
stimulant, a monstrous and tragic turn in
human affairs that he had to square with his aims
and teaching. He had had our common awareness of its possibility, and yet when the crash
came it took him, as it took most of us, by surprise. At first he accepted the war as a dire heroic
necessity. This aggression of a military imperialism had to be faced valiantly. That was how
he saw it. Both his sons joined up at the earliest
possible moment, and the school braced itself
up to train its senior boys as officers, to help in
the production of munitions, to produce aviators,
gunners and engineers for the great service of
the war.

The practical quality of the old boys from Oundle became apparent at once. They stepped from laboratory and factory and office into commissions; they returned from all over the world to prepare for the battlefields. By 1918 over a thousand Oundle boys had gone into the fighting services, three had V.C.'s, many had been mentioned in despatches, awarded the Military Cross and the like.

He did his best to find God and creative force in the world convulsion. Here is a part of an address to the Church Parade of the Cadet Corps which shows his very fine and very human struggle to impose a nobility of interpretation upon the grim distressful last stages of the war.

'It is a pleasant thing to wander about these fields and watch the cadets who are told off to instruct their squads. It is a splendid illustration of the power of co-operation in education—where boys and men, or where a community work together, teaching one another, learning one from the other, where all are teachers and scholars, a body of co-workers, helping, encouraging, stimulating each other. This community method is dominant wherever there is a great stirring, *e.g.*

a great call, a great pressing into a new kingdom; wherever there is a great discovery and a new need. The war will establish it in schools.

'And just one word when you go forth from here. You will carry this mutual co-operative spirit with you. You will love your men, take care of their interests, making full use of their individual faculties, and learn to be co-workers with them.

'It is often said that wars will never cease— that they are a necessity—and in a sense this is true. One thing we know quite well, that in all affairs of life *peace* may be simply the peace of death. There is the peace of lifelessness, of in- activity, notwithstanding all its autumnal beauty. There is the quiet peace which changes not, the conventional belief, the conventional kind of round of work, with lack of initiative, of experi- ment, of testing and trials. There is the peace which follows on contentment with things as they are, the peace of death. The land of peace and of convention, and of cruel contentment. The land of dark Satanic mills—as in Blake's imagery. War may come to break up this death- ful peace. So said John Ruskin. I have a letter written to me just when the war broke out. In July 1914 the O.T.C. was inspected by General Birkbeck, and in his speech he expressed his belief that war was coming. On 2nd August, 1914, he wrote to me :—

' "DEAR MR. SANDERSON,— We little thought when I spoke to those boys of yours how near we were to our trial!" and he adds: "These are the words of a peaceful philosopher, Mr. Ruskin, when concluding a series of lectures on War at Woolwich Royal Academy Institution, which may give you comfort. Men talk of peace and plenty, of peace and learning, of peace and civilisation; but I found that those are not the words which the muse of history has coupled together! On her lips the words are Peace and Selfishness, Peace and Sensuality, Peace and Death ! ! ! I learned, in short, that all great nations learned their truth of word and strength of thought in war; that they were taught by war and betrayed by peace—trained by war and deceived by peace —nourished in war and decayed in peace; in a word, that they were born in war and expired in peace."

'This is the prophet's call to arise and awaken out of sleep; to abandon the easy life of routine and routine's belief. It is a call to rise up and breathe life into the dry bones of the past; it is the trumpet blast for active warfare against all things that have become lifeless and dead. It is the herald call for a new army, to build up a new world of active, creative, dynamic Peace.'

§ 2

In April 1918 his eldest son, Roy, died of wounds at Estaires after the battle of the Lys. Loss after loss of boys and trusted colleagues had grieved and distressed him; now came this culminating blow. There had been the closest understanding between father and son; Roy had left engineering to become a master at the Royal Naval College, Osborne, which Sanderson had helped to reconstruct, and more and more had the father looked to his boy as his chosen disciple and possible successor.

On the Whitsunday following Sanderson preached a sermon on the text: 'I will not leave you desolate, I will come unto you.' The notes of the sermon were untidy, and have had to be carefully pieced together, but I think they rise to a very high level of poetry. And when I copy them out I think how the dear sturdy man in his academic gown must have stood up and clung to his desk, after his manner, full of grief and sorrowful memories of the one 'gentle soul,' in particular, and of many other gentle souls, he had lost—clinging to his desk with both hands as he clung to his faith and speaking stoutly.

'Whitsunday—White Sunday—white, pure, untainted—day of consolation—day of inspiration—perhaps the most joyous time of all the year. Spring in its power, life, Spirit of Peace, joy. Everywhere joy—sanctified, subdued. Joy, and peace, and new life in the music, the harmonies and discords, of Nature—here, in the country. The singing of the birds, their twittering, chattering, calling; their excitement; their restful chirping, abandon of joy, peace without alloy—they are friends of the soul. The atmosphere too—the gentleness of it, the life within it and soft warmth of it: freedom, imagination, inspiration are in the air; the wind bloweth where it listeth. Joy, innocent, white, pure, and happy. Happiness too. Life steeped in the sunshine of happiness. The spring, the elasticity, the eutrophy of life: life-creating life; life-giving life. Happiness on every hand mystic, elusive as the forces of Nature. "The wind bloweth where it listeth, and thou hearest the voice thereof, but cannot tell whence it cometh, nor whither it goeth." Happiness! Not freedom from care, or from sorrow, or from sleepless anguish; not freedom from abasement, not even from dark gloom—the accidie of depression—yet nevertheless the increasing sense of the life of love and service, the power of service, the completeness of it. The happiness which breaks ever and again through the clouds of uncertainties, doubts, darknesses of life—revealing it may be, for a moment, the signs of long years of effort—for as life goes on it is given to catch glimpses of the growth of the soul, something of the part the soul has taken in the building of the kingdom. It is in this life of love and service the words of the Master come to us: "I will not leave you desolate, I will come unto you." '

Followed praise of the beauty of work with which his congregation must have been familiar. And then came this concluding passage:—

'And when these days of wrath are passed away, there will be a great battlefield for a new birth. Days of wrath and then a new revelation.

When God came down on the first Pentecost on Mount Sinai, He came amid thunders and lightnings, and in a thick dark cloud—and when the Holy Spirit of God came to the waiting disciples there was a sound of a rushing mighty wind. And it must be so. New birth comes through much sorrow. So we may hope that new theories of life which for a century have been growing towards birth will spring forth out of this great contest in all the lands of the earth. Vast work there will be, and the labourers sadly fewer. The nation is now sending of her very best into the battlefield. There will be great call for new recruits to restore the countries which are devastated—great calls, too, for investigators in all branches of knowledge. Pioneers are now leading the way in research, in mathematics, in science, in industry, in the laws of logic and thought, with new ways of expression in language and art.

'There is the great pressing need of revolution in the laws and relationships in the social life. We may have visions of a regenerated social state, in which courtesy, justice, mercy, the spirit of the gentle knight, will show themselves in change of thought, of belief; we may have visions of communities guided by principles which we hope and believe rule in our great school. Care for the weak; clothing, feeding, housing, medical care for all; a crime to be poor; to be diseased, to be underfed; these regenerations controlled by the true and public spirit at the cost of the community. Laws for reform and redemption, and not for punishment. Each member of the state cared for, as it is our hope each boy of this school is. Great changes—essential to the well-being of a state, and to each member of it. We may have visions that the spirit of chivalry, of kindness, of courtesy, of gentleness, of all that goes to make the "gentle soul" will bring this redemption to the people.'

§ 3

The war turned Sanderson from a successful schoolmaster into an amateur statesman. Life had become intolerable for him unless he could interpret all its present disorders as the wreckage and confusion of the house-breakers preparing the site for a far nobler and better building. He shows himself at times by no means certain that this would ever prove to be the case, but he had the brave man's assurance that with luck and courage there was nothing impossible in the hope that a more splendid human order might be built at last upon this troubled and distressful planet. But for that to happen every possible soul must be stirred, no latent will for order but must be roused and brought into active service. He had no belief in hopeless and irremediable vulgarity. People are mean, base, narrow, implacable, unforgiving, contentious, selfish, competitive, because they have still to see the creative light. Let that but shine upon them and seize them and they would come into their places in that creative treatment of life which ennobles the servant and enriches the giver, which is the true salvation of souls.

He became a propagandist. He felt he had now made good sufficiently in his school. He had established a claim as an able and successful man to go out to able men, to business men, to influential men of all sorts, and tell them the significance of this school of his, this hand-specimen, this assay sample, of what could be done with the world. He went to Chambers of Commerce, to

Rotary Clubs, to Civic Assemblies, to Luncheon gatherings of business men, to tell them of this idea of organisation for service, instead of for profit and possession. He tried to find industrial magnates who would take up the methods of Oundle in productive organisation. He corresponded extensively with such men as, for example, Lord Weir and Sir Alfred Yarrow and Lord Bledisloe. He wanted to see them doing for industrial and agricultural production what he had done for education, reconstructing it upon a basis of corporate service, aiming primarily at creative achievement, setting aside altogether competitive success or the amassing of private wealth as the ends of human activity. Surely they would see how much finer this new objective was, how much fuller and richer it must make their own lives!

When I tell of this search for a kindred spirit among ironmasters and great landlords and the like I am reminded of Confucius and his search for a duke in China, or of Plato or Machiavelli looking for a prince. There is the same belief in the power of a leader and the need of a personal will; the same utter scepticism in any automatic or crowd achievement of good order; once again the schoolmaster sets out to conquer the world. Perhaps some day that perennial attempt will come to fruition, and the schoolmaster will then indeed conquer the world. Perhaps the seeds that Sanderson has sown will presently be germinating in a crop of masterful business men of a new creative type. Perhaps there are Sandersons yet to come, men of energy; each with his individual difference, but all alight with the new conception of man's creative life. Perhaps Oundle may, after all, prove to be the egg of a new world. Oundle may relapse, probably will relapse, but other, more enduring Oundles may follow in other parts of the world. At present all that I can tell is of the message Sanderson was preaching during the last six years of his life.

Here he is, talking to the textile manufacturers of Bradford. This that follows is from his printed address, restrained and pruned, but for the manner of his delivery, the reader should think rather of that sample sermon and the other descriptions I have given of his personal quality.

'I am very much honoured by your invitation to address this important congress, and I am honoured, too, in being permitted to speak on education in this great city of Bradford. For your city stands out very prominently in the annals of education, and its work is well known by all who have watched educational progress.

'You, gentlemen, are concerned with education: you are much concerned with the education which will promote the welfare of the leaders and workers in your industry; and the welfare of the people in your districts. Industrialism has tumbled upon us, and it is an untamed, unruly being, the laws of which are not yet known, and need study. For some thirty-five years—a long spell—I have, in places removed far away from the voices of industry, devoted my time towards the introduction into Public Schools of those Scientific and Technical studies which, as I understand it, lie at the basis of industrial life. I have always had before me the work of organising Technical Subjects so that they might give all that is best to give of spiritual and intellectual training. And our object is to send forth from school boys that will be in sympathy with the work that they have to do, that they will be privileged to do, and to send them forth equipped for it. You have the same purpose. Your wish is that the boys and girls of your country should have every chance of developing into effective workers in the community, and that they should take a zealous intellectual interest in their work— that they should love their work, love to do it well, ever anxious to mount to higher things.

'And one of the difficulties of the immediate future will be to reorganise industrial conditions so that each worker may have the chance of stretching his faculties and of getting the work that will give him reasonably full play for his abilities. The fact that able and clever men are, in the present system, kept too long at work which does not stretch their brains, is a cause of unrest. Fortunately there is a growing consensus of opinion that more freedom for opportunity and for advancement is seriously necessary, and this sympathetic opinion will lead towards a solution. It is also well within the work of a school to promote this sympathy by sending out boys with those intellectual and scientific tastes and knowledge which will react upon themselves and attract them to the workers.

'There are two other questions which I will

mention before I come to the actual work which may be done in schools. One of the main aims of a good school is to see that each boy and girl is cared for, that each one has every opportunity for development. We must not cast out, or send our weak ones away, we must keep them in school —we must find out what kind of work will appeal to them, so that they, too, may move upwards, gain in self-respect, and love their life. And we claim that this is what we would have done in all factories, or in any occupation. It is the essential duty of every nation. We are anxious that no worker should be stunted mentally or physically by the kind of work he has to do. This again is a difficult as it is an urgent problem. It is one which can be studied in schools, and there is no doubt that the attempts of a school to provide avenues of advance for all kinds of boys will tend to bring the right spirit into industrial and agricultural life. . . .'

§ 4

So much for the Bradford discourse. Here is the gist of a discourse given to the Reconstruction Council in London a year later.

'The object of this paper is to describe in practical working terms an organisation of schools which shall be based on a close association with the manifold needs and labours of the community life. At the outset I may say that the proposals will refer—even if not specifically so stated—to all types of schools, from the elementary to the Public Schools. It will be seen that the change needs a change in the ideals which have usually prevailed in schools of the past. In the community life the one urgent thing to be done to-day is to reorganise industry and the conditions of labour. This reorganisation may require quite organic or even anarchic changes—and for these changes the ideals of boys and girls must be changed, and to prepare for this change is the urgent work of the schools.

'Before I come to the proposals for reconstruction of schools, I will state very briefly some facts in industry which are now meeting with acceptance:

'1. Modern industrial life has come in with a tumultuous rush, in a haphazard, ungoverned way, through the activities of forceful, capable, and industrious leaders who have made use of the scientific discoveries of another type of men.

'2. The shrinkage of the world, and the growth of population which followed, has led to fierce competition; and this spirit of competition has ruled everywhere.

'3. In the ungoverned rush for production all sorts of methods are adopted which seem to be justified by their effectiveness. An example is the modern system of efficiency, at first sight captivating to the intellect and the desires, but yet a method which needs very careful study.

'4. Now men are beginning to believe that the first product of industry must be for the worker; that the worker should grow physically, intellectually, spiritually by his work.

'I shall claim that the work in schools should be permeated by Science and by the scientific method and outlook, and it will be found that Science itself does not set all this store on efficiency. Efficiency, I believe, is entirely contained within the first, or quantitative law of Thermo-dynamics. But eutrophy based on the more elusive qualitative law is concerned with the quality which leads to the giving up of life to others. We must see to it that whatever the efficiency may be, the eutrophy of industry be high.

'The principle that the first product of industry must be the worker leads to great organic changes. It will lead to no less a thing than closing down certain productions, certain classes of occupations, certain industries or processes. It will lead to a modification in repetition work; and to adjustments in organisation. I hope to show the bearing of this on our educational methods, and how the ideals implied may bring some help in diagnosing Labour unrest.

'It will be seen that most of the changes needed to-day depend upon international agreements; and a league of nations is essential, not, I think, to end wars, but to make the change from competition to co-operation possible.

'We are concerned to-day with the part education must take in this change of ideals of life. It is not too much to say that without the influence of a reconstructed education the way to change in the ideals of men will be hard to find. The change has to be made from competitive methods and ideals to co-operative methods; from the spirit of dominance to creativeness; and the present system of aristocraticism in schools must give way to democratisation.

'Competition holds sway to-day in industrial life with disastrous results. Every employer of labour feels this, and wrestles, and would be glad of a change, but he is held in the grip of a system. Every one feels that competition destroys the creative, inventive life—and is the seat of unrest. And yet the spirit of competition holds sway, not in commerce only nor in diplomacy, but in the schools. Our public schools are professedly schools for training a dominant class; the aims, the educational methods, the school subjects and their relative values, the books read, the life led— are all based on this spirit. The methods are largely competitive, possessive. With, as I believe, tragic results in industrial life this same system, with the ideals behind it, has been unwittingly impressed on the working class in the elementary schools. . . .

'The change which I am advocating will demand a new organisation, and will call for a new type of school buildings, and new values of subjects. The new-comer Science, and with it organised industry, which springs out of it, must take a prominent and inspiriting place in school, and in every part of school work. It is not sufficient to say that Science should be taught in schools. The time has gone by for this. We claim that scientific thought should be the inspiring spirit in school life. Science is essentially creative and co-operative, its outlook is onwards towards change, it means searching for the truth, it demands research and experiment, and does not rest on authority. Under this new spirit all history, literature, art, and even languages should be rewritten.

'A new type of school buildings and requirements will arise. No longer buildings comprised only of class-rooms, but large and spacious work-rooms. Class-rooms are places where boys go to be taught. They are tool-sharpening rooms—necessary, but subsidiary. For research and co-operative creative work the larger halls are needed. Spacious engineering and wood-working shops, well supplied with all kinds of machine tools, a smithy, a foundry, a carpenter's shop, a drawing office—all carried on for manufacturing purposes.   Plenty of work which will employ boys of all ages will be found to do.

'There will be a corresponding spacious literary and historical workshop with a really spacious library full of books: books on modern subjects, as well as reference books.   The building should have wings in it for foreign books—modern as well as classic, history, economics, literary, scientific.   As many as possible of the foreign languages should be represented here, that boys may grow up with knowledge and sympathy and respect for other nations, and thus aid in promoting wider and deeper ideals of life. Another gallery for geography, and natural history, travels, ethnology.

'Here is full scope for a large number of boys of all ages to be engaged in research.   It is all of a co-operative character.   They can study the various social and economic systems—from co-partnership to syndicalism; or the Liberation of Slaves; or the League of Nations; or the Liberation of Italy.

'Another block will be a science block with an engineering laboratory, machinery hall, physical, chemical, and biological laboratories—well supplied with apparatus and plant for applied science; plant, too, to lead to the investigations of the day; testing machine, ship tank, air tunnel; a miniature standardising laboratory; and with this a botanical garden and an experimental farm.

'Another would be an art-room, music-room, theatre, a home of industry for studying industrial development and industrial life.

'This is not a Utopian scheme, but one within possibility in town and country. To each large central high school should be associated groups of elementary schools, and there should be free highways between them, neither barred by examinations nor barred by expense. . . .

'Another change must also come. Books on modern problems, strangely enough, are not yet read in schools. For example, the time is overdue for a change in the English books: Burke's *Reflections* and Pitt's *War Speeches*, or Addison, to Ruskin's *Unto This Last* and *Time and Tide*, or to Bernard Shaw, Wells, Galsworthy, and the modern poets. Some would go so far as to give Shakespeare a rest. It is astonishing how the newer books bearing on the large questions of the day, and bearing on the actual life of the boy, strike the imagination of boys—even quite young boys of the upper elementary school age. They stir up the faculties and appeal to a less used kind of imagination. It is surprising, too, what open and live views young boys will reach. And one thing the study of these books possesses, which I hope to dwell upon later, is that they bring the schools into close touch with the every-day life of their homes and of the community.

'Creative education demands that schools should be brought into harmony with the community life, and should take part in the industrial and economic life. When boys and girls go home from school (even to the humblest home) the parents should find there is something their children have done at school which will help them in their work. This means that technical and vocational training should hold a prominent, and not a subsidiary, place in the schools. It is not difficult to see that this kind of work contains within it the spirit and genius of Science. We claim that education should be turned in this direction, with confidence and inspiration. The divorce of industrial life from the life of the spirit is one of the tragedies of the age. It produces calamitous results. A man's work may be of an impossible kind, it may be sordid and destructive of life—and the cure proposed is that he should have shorter hours and more pay. This leads to bad diagnosis of the cause of the Labour difficulty, and prevents necessary reforms in the industries. . . .

'Creativeness, the co-operative spirit and method, the vision, the experimental method of searching for the truth, form the unique gift Science and Industry have to give to the "New Education." Under the influence of this new outlook all other departments of knowledge must be restudied. Under its influence the life of school will become active, the workers self-reliant, love abounding. It will make good craftsmen and make the school of use in the community—whether in the manufacturing life or in the investigation of economic conditions. Incidentally it will give rise to a new body of men capable of going wholly or in part to teaching, and the school will be thus linked up with the life of the place.

'It may be well to state that with an education of this kind based fundamentally on Science a capable boy will leave a secondary school with a good knowledge of Science and of its application, with a research attitude towards history and modern problems, and with a good working knowledge of two, or three, or even four languages. . . .

'The study of social questions is seriously needed. Industries would then have a close connection with the boys and girls, and yet boys and girls would be free to follow the best of their own talents and inclinations—the industrial life would not be separated from the spiritual life; and we may hope that some part of this ideal would pass over into the workshops and factories; so that the labourer would learn to love his work better than his wage—for so indeed he would wish to do. And the faculties of the worker would grow. The method of the work would follow the method of the school, as it is doing more and more in our own land and in many a workshop. For the spirit is with these ideals; the practice difficult for any single firm to carry out. Hence is the need for radical change in schools. Firms are being driven to start trade schools of their own, when they would prefer the work to be done with all the wider scope of a school. And the same enlightened firms endeavour to "promote" their men.

'And here we come to what is probably the natural source of all labour "unrest"—the unstretched faculties of the worker. Men there are in any great shops who have intellectual faculties of the highest order, and these faculties are not used, so the greatest possession a man has, and the greatest his country has—the "faculties" of its owners—is allowed to dissipate. And in the feeling of the mental want of equilibrium, in the slow frittering away of life, there arrives the turbulent spirit. The study of these questions is the problem for our coming international university. The industrial and economic problems involved can only be approached under international agreement. All that has been possible at present in the way of making industrial life pure and holy is by legislative restrictions, often enough rankling to the worker even when needed for his amelioration. Such legislation (Factory Acts, Insurance Acts, wages, hours) does not remove the source of the disease; at best it only mitigates the worst results. More drastic changes may be needed in the nature of the work—to the ruling out certain manufacturing processes until new discoveries can be made.

'So with the work in the shops. Men do not want wages, or shorter hours; these demands are only symptoms of a disease; short cuts to amelioration. They are doctoring. What men want is that their work may be such that they can love it, and want more of it. They do not want slaves' work in the shops and a "dose" of the spiritual life out of it. So we believe.

'Parents, too, would let their children remain at school. As a class there is no one more unselfish and self-sacrificing and co-operative than the working-class parent. Boys want to leave school because of the natural urge for making something and getting to business—as they see it at home. To remain at school without joining in some work is unthinkable when they see the life their parents lead.

'I may be permitted to insert one paragraph on the unfortunate opposition to this new position which is claimed for Science in the schools. The opposition springs from the belief that vocational work is simply material, having no spiritual outlook. But the truth is all the other way. Unfortunately the present studies of history, art, economy, literature, are biassed by "possessive" instincts and education, and we claim that Science and its methods are seriously demanded for a new reading of these things. However, the opposition finds expression in high quarters. The Workers' Educational Union, acting in sympathy with the Labour view—that vocational studies are to be avoided—practically taboos technical studies. This is reasonable as things are to-day, when a man's work is too often for the profit of others, and for this reason the workers are not in love with their work, and when the day is over they have seen plenty of it; so the best of them go elsewhere for the springs of the spiritual life. But this is all disastrous to individuals and disastrous to progress. What the workers should do is to watch for the spirit in their daily work, for it is the work itself which will hold a man to God—nothing else will.'

§ 5

I have quoted from this London Reconstruction discourse very fully. In the official Life

there are a number of such addresses in which the
student will find the main doctrines of that particular address repeated, varied, amplified, but
as my object in this book is to strip Sanderson's
views down to his essential ideas, I will make
only one further quotation from this propaganda
material here. This is from the notes he arranged
for an address to the Newcastle Rotary Club.
His favourite contrast between the possessive instincts and the creative instincts comes out very
clearly here. Like all the great religious teachers,
Sanderson aims quite clearly at an ultimate com-
munism, to be achieved not by revolution but by
the steady development of a creative spirit in the
world.

'Schools should be miniature copies of the
world we should love to have. Hence our out-
looks and methods must have these aims in mind.
Schoolmasters have great responsibilities. We
should be able to say to a boy, we have en-
deavoured to do such things for you, and we ask
you to go forth, it may be, into your father's
business or factory and do the same to the
workers. Let me illustrate from the workshops.
Workshops in a school are by far the most diffi-

cult things to carry on along the lines I have in mind.   Here are three conditions which must be kept in the shops:—

'(*a*) The work boys are doing should not be for themselves, or exercises to learn by; it must always be work required by the community.

'(*b*) Each boy must have the opportunity of doing all the main operations, and all the operations should be going on in the workshops.

'(*c*) Whenever a boy goes into the shop he should find himself set to work which is up to the hilt of his capacity.   There is no "slithering" down to work which is easy, no unnecessary and automatic repetition, no working for himself but for the community.

'And we can say, and are entitled to say, to the boy, when you go forth into life, perhaps into your father's work or business or profession, you must try to do for your apprentices and workers what we have tried to do for you.   You, too, will try to see that every one has work which exacts their faculties—by which they will grow and develop; you will see to it that they are working directly on behalf of and for the welfare of the community, and not for yourself.

'This is your real duty towards your neighbour. It is a vastly hard thing to do. This duty of believing that others are of the same blood with yourself, and have the same feelings, and loves, and desires and needs, and natural elementary rights; this duty of setting them free to exercise their faculties spaciously that they, too, may get more of life—is the real duty towards your neighbour. It is a hard thing. If you think of the works, the factory, the office, it is a hard thing. It involves vast sacrifice—the hardest sacrifice—the sacrifice of belief and economic tradition. We need not be surprised that Christianity has "slithered down" to an easier and softer level of culture and duty towards our neighbours. But whether the workers know it or not, this hard duty is essential in considering the relationships of our community system and our international system to-day.

'It is a hard duty, and boys must be immersed in it in school. The outlook, values, and organisation of a school should be based on the fundamental fact of the community service. By habit of mind, and by the activity of the schools, boys should be imbued with this high duty. It means a reorganisation of methods and aims.

'It is a hard duty, this duty towards your neighbour—the hardest part being to believe that he has like feelings with yourself and equal rights. The young man went away sorrowful, for he had great riches—riches intellectual or other. Yet the young man went away sorrowful, and there is no doubt that he eventually sold all that he had. This is Watts' version of it. The young man was at heart a follower of Jesus; he did not say that the commandment was an old one and well known, that it had been said before in the Hagadah and by Moses; he did not say that the language was the language of Plato or Philo; he did not say that it was too difficult and could not be true for every one—he went away sorrowful. We have no doubt that he sold all that he had.

'The system of education in the past has been based on training for leadership, *i.e.* for a master class, and its method has been a training of the faculties. But the sharply defined line between the leaders and the led has been broken down. The whole mass of people has been aroused towards intellectual creative efforts. The struggle going on in all communities and amongst all races is a struggle to grow and have more of life. Whether at home amongst our workers, or in India, or Egypt, or Ireland; or between China and Europe—the struggle is the same. It is a struggle to make progress, and have more of life. This urge to grow is a biological fact. We cannot tell why it is or what creates it—but everything around us has this urge to grow, and to grow in its own particular way. One seed grows into a tulip, another into wheat. We know not how, but we recognise it. And it is precisely the same urge to grow that is causing all this apparent conflict. It is the fundamental creative instinct ˑ—the most powerful instinct of the human race, by which the race is preserved. Deep down in human nature lies this instinct; it is never forgotten, it is always present in the mind. It is voluptuous, anarchic, joyful, violent, powerful.

'The other instinct is called the fighting, aggressive, acquisitive, possessive instinct. It is the instinct to acquire, to overcome. It is distinct from the creative instinct even in the biological growth, but the distinction manifests itself more clearly in the community or herd relationships. It has none of the beautiful and life-giving qualities of the creative urge.   It is essentially, even in its romance (of which we have plenty), dull, selfish, destructive.   It varies its forms from sheer animal force to the dialectical methods which have assumed the names of talent and culture.   The same characteristics are seen in the force of the slave-driver, in the forces of the wage-nexus, and in the dialectical force of the council.   These are hard sayings, but for the solution of the problems of the present times it is wise, and necessary, to look facts in the face. At any rate it is well to know of the possibilities, feelings, and loves of the uprising mass. . . .

'But what has this to do with schools?   My answer is that if we are to deal with the problems thrown up by science in our industrial system, and our close national and international contacts, the schools must be the seed grounds of the new thought and visions. . . .'

CHAPTER VII

THE HOUSE OF VISION AND THE SCHOOL CHAPEL

§ 1

I COME now to one of the most curious and
characteristic things in Sanderson's later
life, a conflict and interaction that went on
between two closely related and yet in many ways
intensely competitive ideas, the idea on the one
hand of a new sort of building unprecedented
among schools, a building which should symbolise
and embody the whole aim of the school and the
renewed community of which it is the germ, and
on the other hand the idea of a great memorial
chapel to commemorate the sacrifice of those who
had fallen in the war. These ideas assumed
protean forms in his mind, they grew, they
blended and separated again. I will call the first,
for reasons that will appear later, the House of
Vision; the second, the school chapel. For though

Oundle had thrown up a great cluster of houses, halls, laboratories, and other buildings during its quarter of a century of growth, it had never yet produced anything more than a corrugated-iron meeting-house for its religious services. The want of some more dignified chapel had long been evident, and even before the war was very much in Sanderson's mind.

The idea of a House of Vision was therefore the later of the two. Very early in the war a boy of great promise, Eric Yarrow, the son of Sir Alfred Yarrow, the great shipbuilder, was killed at Ypres, and parent and schoolmaster met at the house of the former to mourn their common loss. Sanderson and Eric Yarrow had been close friends; they had discussed and developed the idea of a creative reconstruction of industry together; Eric Yarrow was to have played a part in the industrial world similar to the part that Roy Sanderson was to have played in the educational world.

The two men sat late at night and talked of these vanished hopes. Could not something be done, they asked, to record at least the spirit of these fine intentions, and they sketched out a

Page 90

Catch the contagion of effort
Learning is not our object but
doing.

Page 119

Eutrophy   Page 124

To remain at school without joining
in some work is unthinkable
when they see the life their parents
lead.

project for a memorial building that should be
a symbol and incitement to effort for the reorganised industrial state. It should be in a sense
a museum containing a record of human effort
and invention in the past; a museum of the development of work and production and a state-
ment of the economic problems before mankind.
Sir Alfred produced a cheque more than sufficient
to cover the building of such a memorial as they
had planned, and Sanderson returned to Oundle
to put the realisation of the project in hand.
Probably the two of them also discussed the need
for a memorial chapel and probably neither of
them realised a possible clash between that older
project and the new one they were now starting.

It was in the early stage when the Eric Yarrow
memorial was to be nothing more than a museum of industrial history and organisation that
Sanderson set afoot the building at Oundle which
is now known by that name. Apparently he did
not get much inspiration over to the architect,
and at any rate the edifice that presently rose
was a very weak and dull-looking one, more
suitable for a herbarium or a minor lecture-hall
than for a temple of creative dreams. It was a

premature materialisation, done in the stress and under the cramping limitations of war time. Long before it was finished Sanderson's imaginations had outgrown it. I think this unconfessed architectural disappointment probably played a large part in the subsequent development of the idea of the school chapel, still to be planned, still capable of being made a spacious and beautiful building. To the latter dream he transferred more and more of the ideas that arose properly out of the germ of the Eric Yarrow memorial.

At first the House of Vision was to have been no more than an industrial museum. It was not to be used as a class-room or lecture-room. It was to be empty of chairs, desks, and the like, and clear for any one to go in to think and dream. About its walls, diagrams and charts were to display the progress of man from the sub-human to his present phase of futile power and hope. There were to be time-charts of the whole process of history, and a few of these have been made. As his idea ripened it broadened. The memorial ceased to be a symbol merely of industrial reorganisation and progress, and became a temple to the whole human adventure.

He began to stress first social and then imaginative growth. The charts were to be full and accurate, everything shown was to be precisely true, but there was to be no teaching in the building, no direction beyond the form and spirit of the place.

And so while the scaffolds of the workmen rose about the commonplace little erection in the school fields, the schoolmaster in his day-dreams realised more and more the full measure of the opportunity he was missing.

The realisation of the past is the realisation of the future, and it was an easy transition to pass to the idea of this building as an expression of the creative will in man. In it the individual boy was to realise the aim of the school and of schooling and living. It was to be the eye of the school, its soul, its headlight.

The idea of this 'House of Vision' was still growing in his mind when he died. He had not yet settled upon a name for it, though he had tried over a number of names—a House of Vision, which is the name we have taken for it here, the Home of Silence, the Hall of Industry, the Anthropaeum, the Making of Man, the Life

Creative, the Soul of the School. All these names converge upon the end he was seeking. This approach by trial, by leaving the idea to shape itself for a time and then taking it up again, by talking it over with this man and that, was very characteristic of his mental processes.

A member of the staff recalls a stage in the development of the idea. 'I talked with the head-master about the Yarrow Memorial in October 1920,' he says. 'He then seemed to dally with a suggestion to name it the "Temple of the World" —he expressed his hatred of the tendency to call it the "Museum." I gathered that his idea was to fill it with charts of all things and all ages, including pictures of at least all the world's great men—then to turn a boy loose in it, thereby to realise his position in the world as a unit of its time, as opposed to the inculcation of any idea of his having a part in his nationality only. His root idea seemed to be that it should be a place for meditation—restful as well as invigorating.'

Here is a passage written by Sanderson himself a little later. The idea ripens and broadens out very manifestly.

'Every school, every locality and industry,' he

writes, 'might build within their boundaries a new kind of chapel, a heritage, a temple—a beautiful building in which are gathered together and exhibited the records of man's great deeds and of man's progress, and the records of his needs. It is such a "Hall of Needs" that we regard the Yarrow Memorial, and to this end it is being equipped.'

And here Sanderson speaks again in a sermon preached upon the text of Moses' withdrawal to the mount.

'A school will grow into a book. It will take upon itself the form of a Bible. Within it will appear the stages in the life of the soul—"the coming of a kingdom"; the foundations, the building, the furniture, the complex apparatus, the organised beauty. A school—its buildings, workshops, class-rooms, and all that goes towards a great school—can take on the form of a parable. As we wander from one place to another all that speaks of life will manifest itself before us. How life begins, what is needed for its growth; what shall be its standards, its ideals; what the nature of its proof-plate; the craftsman and what he is;

the craftsman in languages, in mathematics, in science, in art; the secrets of nature revealing themselves; progress, change, vision.

'And boys will go out into the factory, or mine, or business, or profession, imbued with the spirit of the active love of humanity. Some will be called to lead, as Moses was called. They, too, will plant the "Tent of Meeting," the "Temple of Vision." A return with a new view-point will be made to the temple of ages gone by. The Assyrian frescoed his walls with sculptures of the deeds of his hero-kings; the Franciscans frescoed the walls of their chapels with the life of Jesus as told in the Gospels—the life of the Divine builder, of Him who came to restore a kingdom, by whose life and death a new world was created.

'But the Temple of Vision of to-day; the new Tent of Meeting. What of it? The new home of vision will be frescoed with the thoughts of to-day, changing into the thoughts of to-morrow. Generations of workers will go up into the mount, and to them, too, will be shown the pattern. "See that thou make them after their pattern which hath been shown thee in the mount." '

§ 2

Now this is a very great and novel idea, the idea of a modern temple set like a miner's lantern in the forefront of school or college to light its task in the world. It rounds off and completes Sanderson's vision of a modern school; it is logically essential to that vision. But meanwhile what was happening to the school-chapel project?

For, after all, in the older type of school, the chapel with its matins and evensong, its *Onward Christian Soldiers* and suchlike stirring hymns, its confirmations and first communions, was in a rather dreamy, formless mechanical way undertaking to do precisely what the new House of Vision was also to do, that is, to give a direction to the whole subsequent life. But was it the same direction? The normal school-chapel points up —not very effectively one feels; the House of Vision was to point onward. Sanderson had a crowded, capacious mind, but sooner or later the question behind these two discrepant objectives, whether men are to live for heaven or for creation, was bound to have come to an issue.

His mental process was at first syncretic. He began to think of a school-chapel, not as a place for formal services but as a place of meditation and resolve. He began to speak of the chapel also as though it was to be 'the tent on the mount,' the place of vision. He betrayed a growing hostility to the intoned prayers, the trite responses, the tuneful empty hymns, the Anglican vacuity of the normal chapel procedure. Had he lived to guide the building of Oundle chapel I believe it would have diverged more and more from any precedent, more and more in the direction of that House of Vision, that the premature and insufficient Eric Yarrow building had so pitifully failed to realise.

Here is evidence of that divergence in a passage from a sermon preached after a gathering of parents and old boys in the Court Room at the London Grocers' Hall to discuss the chapel project. I ask any one trained in the services of the Church of England and accustomed to enter, pray into a silk hat, deposit it under the seat, sit down, stand up, bow, genuflect, kneel decorously on a hassock, sing, repeat responses, and go through the simple and wholesome Swedish exercises of the Anglican prayer book, what is to be thought of this project of a chapel with hardly a sitting in it? And what is to be thought of this suggestion of wandering round the aisles? And what is this talk of young gentlemen who have died 'for king and country,' casting down their lives for the rescue of man?

'For the years to come, when the war is over, it will be well to have some visible memorial; some symbol of the redemption of the Great War, and of the heroic part old boys have taken in it; some record of the great struggle from out of which the new spirit will rise; some record of the part the whole school took in this; some record of the boys who have fallen; some thanksgiving symbol for all who have given their service. And for this it is proposed to build a chapel. But when the time comes we shall be sad to leave our present building. It is a poor building, but it is very rich in its associations. The services in this temporary chapel have taken a large part in the building of the school. Simple as is the Tent in the Wilderness, yet we have hoped that the Spirit of God would come and dwell in it. We have hoped that the Divine Spirit would come into all the activities and outlook of the school in its diverse occupations, whether they be literary or whether they be scientific or technical. And we have always looked onward to the day when a permanent chapel should be built, symbolic of the Divine Omnipresence for worship and for sacrifice.

'And this is what is in mind to do—and yet I confess to a certain amount of fear. A lofty, spacious chapel I have had no doubt would at the right moment be built by the Grocers' Company. Just before the war the building of this chapel was emerging as the next great building to undertake—a chapel, such as a college chapel with stalls, as for private service. But now we look beyond this. We want something different, more open. A lofty, spacious chapel to form the nave —no fixed seats, the clear open space; quiet, still, "urgent with beauty." Joined to this the choir and sanctuary, with aisles round the three sides of it, forming an ambulatory. Round these aisles, on the walls and in the windows, the recorded memory of the boys who have fallen. An east window, a reredos, stalls, altar. A chapel, abundant in space, not for the mind to sit down in, but for the mind to move about in, for contemplation, for dwelling in the infinite, for

piercing through the night, for vision, for the
clear spirit of thankfulness, for communion with
the saints, our own young saints among them.
So we hope. As you wander round the aisles
there will pass before you the memorial of those
boys who have cast down their lives for the
rescue of man.'

§ 3

I cannot guess how Sanderson, had he lived,
would have resolved this conflict between his
House of Vision and his Great Chapel, just as I
can hazard no opinion of the ultimate form his
interpretation of Christianity would have taken.
But the recognition of these conflicts is fundamental to my conception of the man and his
significance.

He stands for a great multitude reluctant to
abandon many of the familiar phrases of the
Christian use and eager to read new and deeper
meanings into them. But he never took 'holy
orders'; he knew the days of the priest, except
for evil, were past, and it is only by its being born
again as a House of Vision that he could antic-

ipate his chapel with contentment. The time has come for mankind to choose plainly between the priest and the teacher.

Some six months after Sanderson's death I went to Oundle and visited the Yarrow Memorial, that abortive first House of Vision. Except for a bronze statue of a boy by Lady Scott that Sanderson had liked and bought, it was as I had seen it with Sanderson a year before. It was still, deserted, and I suppose I must count it dead. The time-charts had not been carried on. The collection of inventions, the display of humanity's growth, were still represented by empty cases. The statue was intended for the school chapel, but meanwhile it had been dumped in the House of Vision as a convenient vacant place for such dumping. The bronze boy is in an eager pose; there is duty to be done and danger to be faced and a great creative effort to be made. 'Send me!' he said, in that empty, neglected House of Vision. But the hand that would have put that dart to the bowstring and aimed it at work and service was there no more.

Building operations upon the chapel were proceeding slowly. The rising walls were very like the rising walls of the sort of church for respectable people that gets built in Surbiton or Beckenham. I gather that in all probability it will even carry the debt customary in such cases. The new headmaster was, I found, a thoroughly pleasant man who came not from an elementary school but from Eton, and had never met Sanderson in his life and knew nothing of his work. He seemed disposed to regard Sanderson as a bit of a crank and to be intelligently puzzled by his originalities. I felt assured that when at last that old corrugated-iron building is abandoned for the new chapel there would be pews in the new nave in spite of Sanderson, and services of an altogether normal type and no nonsense of walking about and thinking or anything of that sort.

But though I have seen the House of Vision at Oundle dead and vacant as a museum skull, yet I know surely that neither Sanderson nor his House of Vision are in any real sense dead at all. A day will certainly come when his name will be honoured above all other contemporary schoolmasters as the precursor of a new age in education and human affairs. In that age of realisation every village will be dominated by its school,

with its library and theatre, its laboratories and
gymnasium, every town will converge upon its
cluster of schools and colleges, its research buildings and the like, and it will have its Great
Chapel, its House of Vision as its crown and
symbol even as the cathedral was the crown and
symbol of the being and devotion of the medieval
city. And therein Sanderson's stout hopefulness
and pioneer thrustings will be kept in remem-
brance by generations that have come up to the
pitch of understanding him.

CHAPTER VIII

THE LAST LECTURE

§ 1

SANDERSON'S propaganda of this idea of the possible reorganisation of the world through schools came to an abrupt end in the summer of 1922. He died suddenly of heart failure in the Botanical Theatre of University College, London, at the end of an address to the National Union of Scientific Workers. He had chosen as the title of the address, 'The Duty and Service of Science in the New Era,' and it was in effect a recapitulation of his most characteristic views. He attached considerable importance to the delivery and he made unusual preparations for it.

Upon his desk after his death seven separate drafts, and they were all very full drafts, of this address were found. In the margins of the pages little sums have been worked out—so many pages

147

at three hundred words a page, four thousand, five thousand words; a full hour's talking, and still so much to say! There are little notes framed in a sort of Oxford frame of lines reminding him, for example, to 'say more of bringing scientific method into *all* parts of school.' On the reverse of the pages of manuscript are trial restatements. He tried back several times to a fresh beginning. There is a page headed 'The New School,' and giving three headings: the first, which he afterwards marked as second, is, 'The faculty of each member shall be developed'; the second, which became the first, is 'Community service—no competition'; the third is, *'Outlook—aim*, more value than ability. Service. All are equal. The Spirit and the Bride say, Come. Let all that will, come.'

Then we find him trying over his ideas about science under a heading, 'What we claim for science.' Under that are a number of interesting subheads:—

'Its own value in the great discoveries.

'That its spirit is that of life, giving, changing, searching. (Marginal note:—without being deterred by any of the results which may follow.)

'It is "natural" to the vast number of boys.

'Very directly applicable to needs.

'That it has a language and a message. (Marginal note:—it seeks to test, to create new standards, to fearlessly rewrite knowledge.)

'The same spirit.   (? as Christianity: Editor.)

Finally he produced a draft which was at least his eighth. This he had printed and this he may have intended to read to the meeting. But he did not do so. In the end he spoke from a fresh set of notes, which must have been at least the ninth draft. That eighth draft is given in full in the official Life.

His health had not been good for some time, and he kept this lecture and his exceptional interest in it more or less secret from his wife. He spent a long and interested morning at the experimental farm at Rothamsted, and in the afternoon he went to the opticians to get a new pair of spectacles and attended to other small businesses. He met a small party of us at the London University Club in Gower Street to take tea before lecturing. Sir Richard Gregory, the editor of *Nature*, was present, Major Church, the secretary of the National Union of Scientific Workers, and Dr. Charles Singer, the historian of classical science. Sanderson was evidently hot and rather tired, but he did not seem to be ill; he gossiped pleasantly with us and showed us his new spectacles. They were made of a recently discovered glass, opaque to ultra-violet rays and he betrayed the pride and interest of a boy in possessing them.

University College was not very far away, but he asked for a cab thither because he felt fagged. The audience was already assembled and he went straight on to the platform. The present writer made a few introductory remarks, and the lecture began. It is a matter of keen regret to all of us that we allowed him to stand throughout his discourse. It would have been so easy to have arranged for him to talk from a chair; the Botanical Theatre is not a large one and it is quite conceivable that he might be alive now, if one of us could have had that much thoughtfulness for him. We had thought of it—ten minutes after his death.

But we were all so used to the quality of effort in his voice, so accustomed to its sudden fall into almost inaudible asides, that we did not mark what hung over us until the very moment of catastrophe.   His sentences seemed to me a little more broken than usual; he was rather more disconnected, he was leaving rather more than usual to the intelligence of his audience, and as he talked I watched the faces before me rather anxiously to see just how much they missed of what he was trying to get over to them.   He got over much more than I supposed, for I have since talked with many who were present.   A fairly full shorthand note was made at the time, and on this the following rendering of the last address is based.   Like everything that has been printed of his here, it has been clipped and shorn, little distracting side glances have been eliminated and broken sentences filled in and rounded off.

§ 2

'It is a great honour,' he began, 'to come and address scientific workers (I have only recently discovered my claim to be a scientific worker), and to describe to you what has turned out to be a scientific experiment. I hope to show the results of an experiment carried on, not in a scientific laboratory so-called—physical, chemical, biological, or anthropological—but in a school for boys.

'Before doing that, I should like to say that we scientific workers do very much depend on having a number of us together. One scientific worker placed in charge of any great work finds it difficult; scientific workers do not get the chance of appointing men in sympathy with themselves often enough; so it is frequently said that scientific men placed in command of a factory in industry or a department of state at home or in the colonies fail. Well, if so, they fail because scientific men have not often got the opportunity of getting men of like sympathy to work with them. I take it that the object of the National Union of Scientific Workers is to get scientific men with scientific views of life and experimental experience to join together in some great work. When I speak of the duty and service of science in the new era, I mean that I want scientific men to claim justly a larger share in the work of the world, and not to confine themselves to what is called purely scientific work. We want them to expand themselves over a wider area. As a matter of fact, that is what two distinguished writers have suggested: that the time has come when the ordinary discoveries and inventions of science should be closed down in order to enable scientific minds to do this simple thing. Practically everything that exists now is the work of scientific men, their discoveries and their inventions. The whole world teems with the results of the work of science. The great machines we see used in industry—the industrial machine itself—have been created by men of science. Now, I put it to you that when motor cars came in, the nobility of the land found their coachmen of little use. The scientific machine requires scientific men to manage it. Our industrial life is imperfectly organised; all our troubles are due to the fact that we have a process created by science, but organised in the old way by men of a different outlook. The discoveries of science have rushed into the world a considerable amount of unexpected ability. Working men engaged in industrial pursuits have had their intelligence discovered and brought out, and it is one thing to control a mass of human beings who are not thus inspired with the knowledge of their own possibilities, and another to control those who are. It is like trying to control a set of live molecules. It is one thing to control a hard atom and another to control a live electron.

'So that the duty and service of science would seem to lie in scientific men bringing their ideal of life, their standards, their vision, their outlook, and their methods to organise the great machine that their inventions have created. You cannot have a world half scientific and the other half nothing of the sort.

'That is to say, scientific workers will have to consider the whole question, for instance, of economics. I heard yesterday a distinguished member of the Government saying that we cannot change economics. Of course, that is one thing scientific men have got to do, to change economics so that the system of our industry shall be re-created. The system of management by dual control of the master and the slave will not work when the slave becomes an alive, active, intelligent, anarchic being. He will not be governed by the rein but by a system which the magnet can influence. However, the last hundred years has resulted in a race between the changed conditions that science has brought about and the organisation required to control them, in what has been called by Mr. Wells a race between education and catastrophe. In scientific language, it has produced a serious stress because of the hurrying on of change of conditions and the lagging behind of the methods of controlling them. It is this stress, I think, which has broken up the system. You may even say that the war itself is no cause of anything, but a result of the purely automatic action of shearing forces, as when a testing machine breaks a metal bar.

'The end of the war has left us with a whole host of individuals set free, and the business before science men is to organise this new body. It is a big problem, and requires scientific thought, temperament, and outlook to rewrite practically the whole of our knowledge. It reminds me of the tremendous rush there was amongst scientific men to provide workers to overhaul practically everything in biology (and theology) and other parts of human knowledge after the doctrines of Darwin were well established. I take it that all the departments of human life have to be re-

written by men under the influence of the spirit
of science. Our books have to be rewritten, our
very dictionaries. I have often amused myself
with the *Oxford Dictionary*, or found it necessary
to send a boy to that authority for a definition,
and it has pretty nearly always been false. Take
such a simple case as the word "democracy." The
Oxford Dictionary hasn't a thing to tell you about
the meaning of "democracy" as we use it to-day.
It tells you nothing of the living use of words.
That is one of the terrible dangers of leaving our
books in the hands of men who have not got that
outlook which experiment in science brings to the
individual. Consequently I say that the duty of
scientific men is to scour the whole area of knowledge and rewrite it to bring out new standards,
new values, by means of which labour and industry itself, in the first instance, can be reorganised
(the schools first should be reorganised), and then
you can extend it into the wider area of international affairs.

'They tell us that economics cannot change our
human nature. That is the great duty and service
of science—to change human nature. Scientific
men have to collect a band of disciples and make

a new world. As far as I can gather, from a long connection with boys, the only scientific quality which is constant is inertia in response to change. The actual change itself, when it has arrived, no one objects to, and every one says, "Why didn't we do that before?" Scientific workers rarely have their opportunity in industry. To have their full opportunity they are to set forth in the spirit of the Great Master to found a new kingdom: not to manage industry by the standards and values of the present, but to transform them. And they must do what our Master Himself did —collect a faithful band of disciples imbued with the same belief. I know it is freely said (I have been corresponding with some of the leaders in industry) that scientific men cannot do this thing. They can, if only they are true to themselves and their vision; they can absolutely change the whole system under which industry is worked, and change the world to their ideals.

' "Come, and I will make you fishers of men. . . . " The great work that lies before scientific workers to-day is to extend the area of their labours, to become not fishers of facts but fishers of men. There will always be a distinguished band of purely scientific men devoted to pure science, who will abide devoted to pure science; but with the present number trained in science, we claim them also to organise the machinery that science has created. They must leave their ships and nets and become fishers of men. . . . I daresay even scientific workers know that is from the Bible. One of the greatest tragedies scientific men have allowed is for others to steal the Bible from them. The Old and New Testaments, with their record of progressive revelation, form the most scientific book ever seen. Yet scientific men have allowed a certain type of men to steal it from them. Bible stealing is an old thing, and one favourite method is to bind it in morocco and to put it on a top shelf. . . .

'But I must return to my scientific business. When I was at Cambridge I was not regarded as scientific. I was amongst those who took mathematics, and those who took mathematics and classics were respectable and had to attend chapel. But if you inclined at all towards science, or even ethics, you were not supposed to attend chapel. . . .

'I said that I have recently discovered I am a

scientific worker, that I have been working a scientific experiment, though not of the kind accepted for report to the Royal Society. It has been worked by being headmaster of a school for thirty years and by having taught for forty years. When I became a headmaster I began by introducing engineering into the school—applied science. The first effect was that a large number of boys who could not do other things could do that. They began to like their work in school. They began to like school. That led on to introducing a large number of other sciences, such as agricultural chemistry, horse-shoeing (if that is a science), metallurgical chemistry, bio-chemistry, agriculture; and, of course, these new sorts of work interested a large number of other boys of a type different from the type interested in the old work, so we got an exceptional number of boys, curiously enough, unexpectedly liking what they had to do in school. Then I ventured to do something daring; it is most daring to introduce the scientific method of finding out the truth—a dangerous thing—by the process of experiment and research. We began to replace explicit teaching by finding out. We did this first with these newly introduced sciences. Then we began to impress the aims and outlook of science on to other departments of school life. History, for instance: we began to replace the old class-room teaching and learning by a laboratory for history, full of books and other things required in abundance, so that boys in all parts of the school could, for some specific purpose (not to learn; to go into school to learn was egotistical), find out the things we required for to-day. We set them to find out things for the service of science, the service of literature, modern languages, music.

'This began to change the whole organisation of the school, its aims and methods. It was no use organising boys in forms by the ordinary methods of promotion for this sort of work. You have to make up your mind what you have to do, and then go about and collect anybody who would be of service to that particular work. You would require boys of one characteristic and boys of another. You make them up into teams for the particular work they have to do. The boys who do not fit into this or that particular work must have some other particular work found for them. You begin to design the work of the school for them. You must have all the apparatus you want for it, and you must organise for it, but you begin by organising the work for the boys and what they need to find out, and not by putting the boys into the organisation. Now, presently you discover, when you do this, that not a single boy exists who is not wanted for some particular work; to carry out your object every boy is fundamentally equal. One does this, one does that. Each boy has his place in the team, and in his place he is as important as any other boy. Placing them in order of merit does not work any more. The scientific method absolutely changed the position towards class lists and order of merit. That was an astonishing result.

'Another astonishing result was that we could not have anybody who was not working. If a boy was not working, you could see that he was not working. You could see that he was doing nothing. He could not sit at the back of a class-room and seem to be working. Everybody was working. You can manage that in school, but what about the world? All sorts of people may seem to be working and not be working at all. The curate may be doing nothing! (*Chuckle and something inaudible.*) This seems to land us into the extraordinary fact that no community if it is scientifically organised can carry any one who does not do service. I hope you will agree with me that that is scientific.

'A little farther on I turned round on the boys and the parents. (Both are my business.) I said, "I have and the school has tried all it could to see to it that your boy got the right kind of work to do. We spared no trouble or expense to see to it that he might be able to perform his service in the school and to the community. . . . When you go forth to your father's works, keep in mind that it is your business to see to it that every person that comes within your influence has a like opportunity." That is totally different from your duty to your neighbour as taught in the Church Catechism. We have landed ourselves hopelessly in the position of having a practical community definition of our duty towards our neighbour. You remember the rich young ruler who came to ask what his duty was, and went away sorrowful because he had great possessions. Some of these possessions were perhaps intellectual. I like to think of Watts' picture of that man and I like

Watts' idea that he came back. I hope if any of our boys go away they will come back.

'Another step. This actual love of work spreads, and ultimately every one comes within its influence, and they begin to like the service they are rendering. Finally, competition dwindles and passes away, so that we have reached what appears to be a change in human nature. It is not really a change, but by care and attention calling out what has always been ready there in human nature, namely, a first instinctive love to create. I have always held that competition is a secondary interest and creation a primary instinct. Competition dwindles and passes away. Competition is a very feeble incentive to live. It is cheap and easy to arouse the motive, it is a swift motive and on the surface of things ready for you, but it is not even a powerful motive. Half the boys it dispirits and leaves idle and useless.

'The passing of competition leads on to another thing passing away, which is this: you soon find that a body of workers that as a community has attempted to provide for itself, as a community adapts itself to the community spirit, and punishment is totally unnecessary. It was a long time before that dawned on me. I have not, as a headmaster, taken any part in any shape in punishing boys directly, either by the easy methods supposed to train them for after life or by the other methods that have sprung from the fertile brains of a dominant order. Punishment, I declare from years of experience in this experiment, is a crime: not only a crime but a blunder. Why? Because it is a cheap and easy thing. If you punish it is easy, but if a community has so to arrange itself and adapt itself as to produce the reaction on the individual not to do objectionable things, that is hard. It is complicated. It requires an abundance of real sacrifice. It demands readjustment of everything upon a basis of service. I have been much impressed recently by the effect of having punishment organised in removing any activity on the part of the community itself towards adjusting itself so that punishment should not be necessary. I used to flatter myself, "I don't punish that boy, my prefects do; they keep me right." But I have been convinced by my thirty years of experiment that that was all wrong. These things come slowly. Now, without any action on my part, the prefects have stopped punishing, and a good thing for them. If they leave their boots about, the small boys will too, and they will have to punish them for doing so. To leave your own boots about like a lord is a fine thing, and to punish the small boy who does so is also a fine thing! But it is easy. The hard thing is never to leave your own boots about. . . .

'The reactions that we have been taught to make in the world are weakly static. What is the good of static methods? There is friction; we are told how to overcome frictional resistance. We can put an end to friction by stopping the machine. That is the static method of dealing with friction. Or we can go on working the machine, with oil and care . . . which is not so cheap and easy, but which gets somewhere. . . . If we try to remove friction by the static methods of punishment we are removing the incentive to live a dangerous life. "The secret of a joyful life is to live dangerously." You only live danger-ously if you are perpetually trying to overcome your own inertia and trying to get the capacity to do great things. If you are only defensive, static, it is a waste of time. Yet those defences and resistances are securely placed in the governance of the state. What a curious thing is the form of government! Its characteristics include no repentance, no regret, otherwise it would acknowledge itself less than the governed. Its ideal is a perpetual static calm. *Suaviter in modo, fortiter in re.* It is the method of people who perform the confidence trick. It is the method of "If you want peace, prepare for war." . . .'

For some minutes Mr. Sanderson paused. He looked at his notes. He was obviously very fatigued, but very resolute to continue. He read:—

'Acquisitiveness leads to these glorified things: general science, general knowledge, national history, scholarships, examinations, advanced courses, "interesting" things (whoever wanted to be interested?), the theological thing called "syncretism," tact, swindling. . . .'

Mr. Sanderson stopped and smiled in a breathless manner, half panting, half laughing, very characteristic of him. His glasses gleamed at the audience. His smile meant: 'We are going a little too fast, boys. Where are we getting to? Where are we getting to?' He affected to refer to his notes and then broke away upon a new line.

'Out of all these things I have been telling you, out of all these considerations, evolves the modern school. The modern school is not made by the very simple and easy method of abandoning Greek. (Laughter.) Nor is it made by introducing science or engineering. The modern school's business is to impress into the service of man every branch of human knowledge we can get hold of. The modern method in the modern school does not depend on any method of teaching. We hear a great deal about methods of teaching languages, mathematics, science; they are all trivial. The great purpose is to enlist the boys or girls in the service of man to-day and man to-morrow. The method which makes learning easy is waste of time. What boy will succumb to the entreaty: "Come, I will make you clever; it will be so easy for you; you will be able to learn it without an effort"? What they succumb to is service for the community. I have tested that in the workshops. They don't want to make things for themselves; they soon cease to have any longing desire to make anything even for their mothers. What they love to do is to take part in some great work that must be done for the community; some work that goes on beyond them, some great spacious work. You can spread them out into all sorts of spacious things, in all departments, such things as taking part in investigating the truth. The truth, for instance, of the actual condition of the coal-miners or of any miners. An important question which we have been concerned with for at least three years is *"What is China? What is it like?"* You may say, "Methods of teaching geography." But who ever learned anything from geography—as geography? Who wants to know geography—as geography? Books exist for it, maps, plasticine exists for it. We want to know about China. If we are going to see to it that every one of our working men has the same opportunities that in our school we give to our boys we shall have some difficulty with China. We shall never be able to give our working people these opportunities unless the Chinese give them too. Scientific men must find themselves dominant in the Foreign Office and Colonial Service so as to know what is the nature of the people in these distant places, how we can bring to them what we are able to give to our sons—the opportunity of making the highest and best use of their faculties. We shall not get that sort of thing from geography books. You will have to take the boys and let them find out what men have done who have been in China: to get products from China; to know its geology, and whether, after all, the Chinese do so deeply love rice that they want to live on a very little a day. Do the Chinese love rice? Do they love underselling white labour? Do they want to? That is real geography, but not class-room geography. That extension of interest, until China is brought into the class-room and the boys are finding out about it, is, I claim, one of the deepest and greatest tasks to be undertaken. China—India—the Durham miners—spacious undertakings. . . .

'Schools must be equipped spaciously, *spaciously*, and they must have a spacious staff. I have the list of our staff here. We have masters for mathematics, physics, chemistry, mechanics, biology, zoology, anthropology, botany, geology, architecture, classics, history, literature, geography, archaeology, economics, French, German, Spanish, Italian, Russian, Eastern languages, art, applied art, handicrafts, and music.

' "Impossible," some people say. There is no

great school in the land but could quite well afford it. . . .

'We must send out workers imbued with the determination to seek and investigate truth—truth that will make them free—and to take great care that in the search for truth they will never take part in or sympathise with those methods by which the edge of truth is blunted.'

§ 3

The voice beside me stopped. Some one pushed up a chair for Sanderson and he sat down. There was applause. I stood up and then struck by a thought, whispered: 'Would you like to answer a few questions?'

'Yes, yes. Certainly,' he said.

'Not too tired to answer them?'

'No—no.'

I had a little strip of notes in my hand and I thought of underlining one or two points in this tremendous project of a school he had spread before his audience before I let in the questioners. I began by saying that the lecture had been a little hard to follow but that it would repay following into the remotest corners of its meaning. Then I heard a little commotion behind me and turned round to see what was the matter. Sanderson had slipped from his chair on to the platform and was lying on his back breathing hoarsely. His collar and tie were removed forthwith. There were several doctors on the platform with us and they set to work upon him. I hesitated for a moment and then declared the meeting at an end, and asked the audience to disperse as speedily as possible. I thought it was an epileptic fit and I had no sense of Sanderson's impending death. I had never seen anything of the sort before. I could not believe it when they told me he was dead.

The windows of the hot and sultry room were opened and most of the people made their way out, but the reporters remained and one or two persons of the curious type who hung about vaguely with an affectation of decorous sympathy. The lecture had been a very difficult one for the newspaper men, and they came now with a certain eagerness to ask questions about Oundle and Sanderson's career. I answered them as well as I could. Sanderson lay across the back of the platform, bare-chested and still. It became evident that I had to seek out Mrs. Sanderson and tell her of this disaster.

There was a little difficulty in ascertaining at which hotel Mr. and Mrs. Sanderson had been staying, and when I got there I found she was out shopping, and I waited some time for her return. Meanwhile her daughter and her daughter-in-law at Oundle were called up by telephone to come to her at once in London. I told her at first that her husband was ill, and then, as we went together in a cab to University College, dangerously ill. She was fully prepared to hear from the doctors at the hospital that the end had come. The poor lady took the news very simply and bravely.

In the Mortuary Chapel of University College Hospital I saw my friend's face for the last time, in all the irresponsive dignity of death. We took Mrs. Sanderson to him and left her for a time alone with him. Four years before in the same London hotel at which she was now solitary, he and she had shared the bitter grief of their eldest son's death together.

§ 4

An event of this sort produces the most various reactions in people, and I recall with a distressful amusement two unknown persons who accosted me as I went out from University College to find a taxi to take me to Mrs. Sanderson. One was a young woman who came up to me and said: 'Don't be grieved for your friend, Mr. Wells. It was a splendid thing to die like that in the midst of life, after giving his message.'

I did not accept these congratulations and I made no reply to her. I was thinking that a little acute observation, a little more consideration on my part, a finer sense of the labour I was putting upon my friend, might have averted his death altogether. And I was by no means convinced that his message was delivered, that it had reached the people I had hoped it would reach and awaken. I had counted on much more from Sanderson. This death seemed to me and still seems far more like frustration than release.

Then presently as I gesticulated for a cab near Gower Street Station, I found a pale-faced, earnest-looking man beside me asking for a moment's speech. 'Mr. Wells,' he said, 'does not this sudden event give you new views of immortality, new lights upon spiritual realities?'

I stared at a sort of greedy excitement in his face. 'None whatever!' I said at last and got into my taxi.

I must confess that to this day I can find in Sanderson's death nothing but irreparable loss. He left much of his work in a state so incomplete that I cannot see how his successors can carry it on. In matters educational he was before all things a practical artist, and education is altogether too much the prey of theories. He filled me—a mere writer, with envious admiration when I saw how he could control and shape things to his will, how he could experiment and learn and how he could use his boys, his governors, his staff, to try out and shape his creative dreams.

He was a strong man and in a very profound and simple way a good man, and it was a very helpful thing to feel oneself his ally. But now that he is gone, now that all his later projects and intentions shrivel and fade and his great school recedes visibly towards the commonplace, I do not know where to turn to do an effective stroke for education. It is only schoolmasters and schoolmistresses and educational authorities and school governors and school promoters and university teachers who can really carry on the work that he began. In this book I have tried to set out as clearly as possible, and largely in his own words, his fundamental ideas of the supersession of competition by co-operation, of the return of schools to real service and of a House of Vision, a Temple of History and the Future, as the brain and centre of community life. This present book is, as it were, a simplified diagram of the teachings less luminously and more fully set out in the official Life.

One thing I shared with Sanderson altogether, and that was our conviction that the present common life of men, at once dull and disorderly, competitive, uncreative, cruelly stupid and stupidly cruel, unless it is to be regarded merely as a necessary phase in the development of a nobler existence, is a thing not worth having, that it does not matter who drops dead or how soon we drop dead out of such a world. Unless there is a more abundant life before mankind, this scheme of space and time is a bad joke beyond our understanding, a flare of vulgarity, an empty laugh, braying across the mysteries. But we two shared the belief that latent in men and perceptible in men is a greater mankind, great enough to make every effort to realise it fully worth while, and to make the whole business of living worth while.

And the way to that realisation lies, we both believed, through thought and through creative effort, through science and art and the school.